The Cou

Overcoming A

By Louise Palmer

Contents

Introduction

This book is based on real-life counseling sessions. The themes are based on real events that occurred during counseling sessions with various clients.

The therapy used is called 'Solution Focused Therapy'. It is a brief therapy that is designed to focus on the resources of the client. It focuses on strengths and aims to help the client become aware of their own solutions through a specific set of questions. It encourages the client to think about the future and only uses the past as a means to identify what works and does not work for the client.

Session One

(The first session is aimed at finding out about the client's concerns and finding out what has helped and what has not helped so far. I want to keep a focus on what has worked so far in the hope of keeping the session positive and solution focused. I had a brief telephone call with the client a week before the session to ask her to notice if there were any positive changes. Many clients, when asked to notice positive changes, can identify at least a few. As the client has started to achieve positive change before the counselor gets involved, it can increase her confidence and help her to appreciate she was already making positive changes before seeking help.)

The first session is taking place at the client's home.

Counselor: Hi. I'm Louise.

Client: Hi come in. Please take a seat in the lounge.

Counselor: Thank you. It's a lovely place you have here.

Client: Thanks. I have recently decorated this room. I spend a lot of time in it and wanted to make it look nice.

Counselor: It's lovely.

Both client and counselor sit down in the lounge.

Counselor: So, I would like to start by telling you a little bit about what will happen during the session.

Client: Okay.

(I want to explain to the client the solution focused approach. I need to get her buy in, in order for the sessions to be effective. I need to set her expectations at the start.)

Counselor: I think it's important for me to grasp what your concerns are and how you would like things to be different. My belief is that you have a lot of strengths and skills that will help you overcome these difficulties. Part of my role is to listen out for these and ask you questions about them. I believe that we can learn a lot from what is working well in our lives and I hope that we can spend time discussing this. I won't be advising you on what you should and shouldn't do. Instead I want to work with you to develop solutions together.

Client: Um, okay. So let me get this straight. You are not going to look into my past?

Counselor: We will look at the past in as much as it will help to identify possible solutions. We will look at what you have tried previously to overcome your concerns and ...

Client: So I don't have to talk about my childhood?

Counselor: No. Not unless you think it will help you.

Client: No! That's a relief! I'm sick of talking about it. It never seems to help anyway. It just upsets me more.

Counselor: I would prefer to focus on the future and solutions. I use a therapy called Solution Focused Therapy. This type of therapy has very good results and it usually much briefer than traditional counseling methods which look into the causes of problems.

Client: Great.

Counselor: You will notice that I will make notes throughout the session. I am not 'analyzing' you. I am merely making notes to aid my memory. At the end of the session I like to summarize what we have covered. Is this all okay with you so far?

Client: Yes. Yes of course.

Counselor: Great. So we spoke briefly on the telephone last week. What are your concerns at the moment?

Client: Well, I suffer with anxiety and panic attacks. The panic attacks are awful. It makes me feel too scared to go out of the house. And I feel bad. I feel bad for my husband. We can't go out like normal couples. If he wants to go somewhere, he has to go on his own. Only last week it was his brother's wedding and I just couldn't make it. I really wanted to go and I just couldn't do it when it came to the day. I should have known that I wouldn't be able to.

Counselor: Okay.

Client: I'm just sick of it, you know? I've had it for 3 years now and I feel like I'm wasting my life. Everyone else is out having a good time and I'm stuck at home doing nothing. Rob, my husband, has been great but I can see he gets frustrated with me sometimes. And that upsets me but I understand it. It can't be easy for him either. I'm just sick of it. I'd do anything to get better. But nothing I try works.

Counselor: So what are your hopes for the work that we do together?

Client: I don't want to feel anxious anymore. I want the panic attacks to stop.

Counselor: What do you want to feel instead of the anxiety?

(It's important that the goal is worded positively rather than negatively. I want to know what the client wants rather than what she doesn't want.)

Client: I want to feel calm. I want to feel that when I go out I can concentrate on having a good time rather than seeing it as an endurance test. I want to be able to just go out and do the simple things like pop to the shop on my own and grab a loaf of bread.

Counselor: You said that at the moment when you go out, you see it as an endurance test. Can you explain what you mean by that?

Client: Yes, sometimes I do manage to go out with my husband. I feel anxious but I grit my teeth and I get through it.

Counselor: What do you think that says about you as a person?

(In this question I am trying to get the client to realize her strengths and resources that can help her to achieve her goals.)

Client: That sometimes I can be really determined. When I put my mind to something I can usually get through it. But that's not always the case. Most of the time I don't even feel strong enough to try.

(The client has finished with a negative statement. I try to turn it back on to focusing on the times when she does feel strong enough to try to go out in the hope that we can learn what helps her to feel strong.)

Counselor: So sometimes you feel strong and determined to go out and you manage the anxiety?

Client: Yes. Yes, I guess I do.

Counselor: What helps you to do that?

Client: Um...I don't know really. Maybe getting a good night's sleep. If I feel tired, I feel more anxious.

Counselor: Getting a good night of sleep helps you to feel strong and determined about managing your anxiety. What else helps?

Client: Hmm. I don't know really.

Counselor: Okay. On a scale of 0 to 10, 10 being completely ready and 0 being not ready at all, how ready are you to start working on overcoming your anxiety?

(I am using scaling questions here. I use them quite a lot. They are very useful in this type of counseling. It gives me a good indication of what the client is feeling and how she can move forward.)

Client: I would say a 10! I am sick of it. I just want it gone! Today I am feeling really determined to fight it.

Counselor: What is making you feel determined to fight it today?

Client: I'm feeling angry about it. I'm ready to go out there and sort this out. It's gone on for too long. I've lost a few friends over it and I'm worried I am going to lose my husband too. I need to sort this out.

Counselor: That's great determination you have there. Now I know a little about your concerns, I would like to know a bit more about you as a person.

Client: Err...okay, what would you like to know?

Counselor: In the free time you have, what do you like to do?

(I want the client and I to engage in some problem-free talk. I am looking for strengths and resources that are needed for her hobbies. Hopefully some of the strengths and resources she uses from her hobbies can be utilized elsewhere.)

Client: Well that's half the problem. I used to love mountain biking and playing tennis but I don't feel up to doing those activities anymore.

Counselor: Are there any hobbies that you still manage to do?

Client: Yes, I like to read. And recently I have started to learn the guitar.

Counselor: That's interesting. How long have you been playing the guitar?

Client: I started about 6 months ago. I am just teaching myself from You Tube at the moment as I can't go out and go to a lesson obviously.

Counselor: What have you learnt so far?

Client: I know my basic chord shapes. I can't move between them very quickly but it's coming slowly. I know I can get there if I just keep practicing. I'm finding it harder than I thought. I thought playing a guitar would be easy.

Counselor: So even though playing the guitar is difficult, more difficult than you first thought, you have managed to persevere?

Client: Yes, I guess so.

Counselor: Do you have any other hobbies?

Client: Yes, I like cooking. I'm not very good at it but I am trying to learn.

Counselor: So you are spending your time at home constructively. You are teaching yourself guitar and teaching yourself how to cook. I think it's great that you are using your time wisely. A lot of people wouldn't do that.

Client: Really? Oh, thanks. Yes I guess I am using my time wisely. Thanks for saying that. Oh, I also try to keep fit by doing aerobics in the lounge - with the curtains shut obviously. People don't need to see that!

Counselor: So even though you are having a difficult time you are resourceful enough to try and make the best of it by engaging in various hobbies you can do.

(Here I am highlighting to the client that even though she is having a difficult time she is being resourceful. Clients aren't often aware how well they are doing. It's about highlighting to them what they are already doing well.)

Client: Yes, I suppose I am. That's pretty good isn't it?

Counselor: Very good. Let's go back to the guitar. What strengths or skills do you have to have when playing the guitar?

Client: Patience! I think a lot of patience. You have to not give up. Keep trying. Keep practicing what you can't do and eventually it starts to get better.

Counselor: What else?

Client: You have to have good rhythm.

Counselor: Do you naturally have good rhythm or is that something you have had to learn?

Client: I have had to learn it.

Counselor: How have you done that?

Client: Just by listening really intently to songs. Counting my beats. I looked it up on the internet and figured out how to count the beats.

Counselor: It sounds like you are very resourceful.

Client: Really? Do you think so?

Counselor: Yes. From what you have told me about your hobbies so far I can see that you are determined, resourceful, patient and you try to make the best of a bad situation.

Client: Wow. I had never really thought of myself that way before.

Counselor: How do you think these strengths could help you feel calmer when you go out?

Client: Hmm... I don't know.

Silence.

Client: I guess the patience one will help. And the determination. I know it can take a long time to get better from anxiety. I have been looking on the internet and some people take years to get better. One person I was reading about had it for 21 years.

Counselor: And what do you know about yourself that tells you that you will not suffer for that long?

(I don't want the client to think that it will take her 21 years to recover. I want her to realize what strengths she has that make her better able to recover.)

Client: Because I'm determined. I am going to fight this. But then just saying that makes me feel scared. I feel too scared to go outside. It's alright me saying all of this to you but when it comes to the crunch, I just can't do it. I just can't. But I want to. But I can't.

Counselor: What in particular made you feel that now was a good time to talk things over?

Client: My husband suggested I should seek help. I have been trying to get myself better for three years now and nothing has helped. To be honest I think he is sick of it. I think he thought I would shake it off in a few months, that it was just a phase or something, but now I think he is getting a bit tired of it all. It can't be easy for him - living with me. I get so upset sometimes. Sometimes I feel like I can't go on. It's just too difficult. Too difficult to face.

I can't believe this has happened to me. I never thought I would get anxious. I'm not that kind of person. Although it turns out I am exactly that kind of person.

Counselor: Anxiety can affect anyone at anytime in their life. You said that you have been trying to get yourself better for three years. What have you tried?

(I want to know what the client has tried in order to find out what has worked and what has not worked. Even if there are small elements of things working we can build on these.)

Client: Deep breathing. They say that all you need to do to stop a panic attack is breathe in and out for four and the panic attack will subside. But it just doesn't work for me at all. It seems to work for everyone else but not for me. If anything, it makes me feel light headed. It makes me feel worse and more panicky.

Counselor: What else have you tried?

Client: Everything. Everything they suggest.

Counselor: Can you give me any examples?

(I need specific examples to work with.)

Client: They say to drop your shoulders, make sure that your body is not tense. That doesn't work either.

Counselor: What else have you tried?

Client: Um. I'm just trying to think. You've put me on the spot now!

Counselor: Take your time.

Client: One thing I read was that you can just imagine yourself walking through the anxiety as if it is a cloud. I don't find any of that visual stuff helpful at all. It just doesn't appeal to me and it doesn't work anyway.

Counselor: Is there anything else that you have tried?

Client: I tried distracting myself and sometimes actually this can work.

Counselor: So distracting yourself can help?

Client: Yes.

Counselor: How do you do that?

Client: Um...I don't know really.

Silence.

(I am using silence here to make the client think. Often by remaining silent the client engages in deeper thought and can then answer a question they couldn't previously).

Client: I try to talk to someone nearby. For example, if I was on a bus I would try to talk to the person next to me. If I can get into a conversation, I find that I am thinking about what they are saying and what I am going to say and that makes the anxiety feel less. It's still there. I can still feel it but it feels a bit better. It can still come in waves though and I can suddenly panic and want to run away and stop talking to the person but ultimately, yea, it helps sometimes.

Counselor: So it helps to distract yourself by talking to someone. How else do you distract yourself?

Client: Err... if there is no one to talk to, I look at my phone. That can help.

Counselor: What do you do on your phone?

Client: I send a text message to a friend or look at Facebook or read the news.

Counselor: Anything else?

Client: Sometimes I play scrabble on my phone! That really takes my mind off things as I have to concentrate, you know, to make up the word with my letters. That helps quite a bit actually.

Counselor: Distracting yourself by talking to someone or looking at your phone helps. Have you found anything else helps to distract you?

Client: Sometimes I ring a friend or my mum. Talking helps. If I am really anxious and I am out, I will ring a friend of mine. She talks incessantly but it is a great way to keep my mind off things.

Counselor: That's great. You have found that distracting yourself can make the anxiety feel more tolerable and you have different strategies to distract you depending on the situation.

(The client and I have discovered a solution. The client has found distracting herself can help. I have kept asking her how she distracts herself in order to gain a number of different ways she can do this. By repeating it back to her, it helps to clarify this in her own mind. Hopefully, the next time she is anxious it will be easier for her to recall all the different things she can do to distract herself.)

Client: Yes but it's not enough. It's not enough to stop me from feeling anxious or being able to cope with the anxiety and feel able to go out like normal.

(This tells me that the distraction technique alone is not enough for the client to manage her anxiety. This is to be expected. It will take some time to discover the different strategies that are right for this client.)

Counselor: If 0 was feeling unable to go out at all and 10 was able to go out like normal, where on the scale would you say you are today?

Client: 3

Counselor: What number would be good enough to get to?

Client: I suppose an 8. If I could go out but still felt a bit anxious, I could deal with that. I would ideally like to be a 10, with no anxiety so that I felt normal though.

Counselor: How will you know that our work together is finished? What will be happening for you?

(It's important that I know where our finish point is. If I didn't, the counseling sessions would be in danger of going on for longer than is necessary. Solution Focused Therapy is designed to be a brief intervention whereby the client does not become dependent on the counselor as in some longer counseling interventions.)

Client: I would be able to go to the local shop on my own. I would be able to cope with my anxiety attacks so even if I did have one, I would know how to cope. I wouldn't feel scared to go out of my front door every day. I'd be socializing with friends again. And maybe I'd start to work again even if it was only a part time job or a voluntary job to begin with. That way I'd know I was on the right track. I'd know that I was getting better.

Counselor: So once you start to socialize with friends, feel ready to start work and know how to manage an anxiety attack you would be happy to end the counseling sessions.

Client: Yes. I think by that point I will have all the tools I need. I will know how to manage the anxiety and I will just be building on what I have learnt. I will be building on what works. I'm not naive. I know I am not going to wake up one morning and suddenly be better. I know that happens for some people but it doesn't seem to happen for me. It looks like I need to work at things.

Counselor: Do you think I know enough to help you? Is there anything else you would like to tell me about?

Client: I just want to let you know that sometimes I feel really down about everything. Like everything is hopeless. Sometimes I wonder if I will be like this for ever. I'm not saying I'm suicidal or anything but I do think I am a little bit depressed. Who wouldn't be in my position? Never being able to go out. I think sometimes it gets on top of me. I'm managing at the moment but sometimes I feel frightened that I will feel lower and lower and sink deeper into depression.

(The client has clearly been having a tough time. I want her to identify some of her coping strategies. Even though it has been difficult she is still managing to cope and therefore has coping strategies that are working. These coping strategies, once identified, can be used to help her to achieve her goals and overcome setbacks.)

Counselor: It sounds like you have been having a difficult time. How are you managing to cope at the moment?

Client: I think I am naturally a hopeful person. Always hoping things will get better. I have bad days, usually two or three bad days in a row when it all feels hopeless. I just spend the days crying. It's really tough on Rob as he hates to see me in such a state.

Counselor: How do you get to the point where you feel like you can cope again? How do you stop feeling so bad and stop crying?

Client: I don't know really. I just get back my determination. I start to feel angry at it again and that helps. I start to want to fight again. It's like I have a cry, get it all out of my system and then I can start again.

Counselor: What are you thinking as you start to get your fight back?

Client: That I can do this. Well, that maybe I can do this. Other people have overcome their anxiety. If they can do it, then I can do it. But then I feel scared and feel I can't do it.

Counselor: Do you remember on the first phone call we had that I asked you to notice if there were any examples of positive change that were already happening in your life?

Client: Yes.

Counselor: What changes did you notice?

Client: I was surprised actually. I did notice a few things which is odd as when you said that, I thought that I wouldn't notice anything.

Counselor: Great. What changes did you notice?

Client: I felt calmer one evening and suggested to my husband that we go for a walk. I never do that. But it was such a lovely summer's evening and it was fairly late, about 9pm. And I just wanted to get out. I felt quite relaxed and we went for a walk.

(Just paying attention to positive changes can impact on the client before she even attends a session. The client can be used to looking for the negative aspects and dismissing the times when her problem is not there or is not there as intensely.)

Counselor: That's good. So you felt calm and quite relaxed, you recognized this and used this as an opportunity to go out for a walk.

(Summarizing this back to the client can help to identify this as something that helped and therefore something that might help again in the future.)

Client: Yes, I guess I did. I felt anxious on the walk, but I coped. It wasn't too bad - the anxiety wasn't too bad. I didn't have a panic attack or anything. It was nice to be outside - and not just in my garden.

Counselor: What helped you to feel calm and relaxed?

Client: I think it was because I wasn't expecting to do it. If I had known in the morning that I was going to go for a walk that evening, I would have fretted all day and probably not have been able to go. That's what I do. I worry myself sick. I know that I make things a lot worse for myself.

Counselor: So going out spontaneously when you haven't had time to worry about it helps you?

Client: Yes.

Counselor: Okay that's good to know. I just want to pause there and check are we talking about what you want to talk about so far in this session?

Client: Yes.

Counselor: Is the conversation helpful so far?

Client: Yep, so far everything is good. It's different to other counseling I have had but it's good. Good different. I don't feel like a crying for a start. If anything, I 'm feeling hopeful.

(Many clients find solution focused therapy quite different to other therapies they have tried. Its positive focus usually ensures that the client is engaged and willing to work with the counselor, rather than feeling criticized and defensive.)

Counselor: Great, I'm really pleased to hear you are feeling hopeful. I want to ask you a particular question now. It's a bit of a strange question but bear with it. Many clients find it helpful.

(I am about to ask the 'miracle' question. This question is a bit odd but it helps to clarify where the client would like to get to. It helps to clarify their

preferred future. This can help with goal setting and usually motivates the client.)

Client: Okay. I'm intrigued now!

Counselor: I want you to imagine that when you go to sleep one night a miracle happens and the problems that you have told me about disappear. You are asleep and therefore you don't know that a miracle has happened. When you wake up in the morning, what would be the first signs for you that a miracle had happened?

Client: Hmm... I'd feel calm. Relaxed. Happy.

Counselor: What would be making you feel calm, relaxed and happy?

Client: My thoughts I guess. I would be thinking 'right'.

Counselor: What would you be thinking?

Client: I wouldn't be thinking about how anxious I am. I wouldn't be worrying.

Counselor: What would you be thinking instead?

(Again, I'm trying to get the client to think about what she would be thinking rather than what she wouldn't be thinking. This can be quite tricky for the client to begin with.)

Client: Oh that's a really difficult one! Umm...

Silence.

Counselor: Take your time.

Client: I don't know really. I don't know what I would think if I wasn't thinking about my anxiety.

(Here I need to change tack. I decide to look at times when she is feeling relaxed.)

Counselor: When are you at your most relaxed?

Client: When I am in the bath and about to go to bed. I've got nothing to worry about then you see.

Counselor: When you are in the bath and about to go to bed, what are you thinking about?

Client: I can't really think. I think I am just in the moment. I'm just enjoying the moment. Not really thinking about anything.

Counselor: So when you are in the moment and just focusing on the here and now, you feel calm.

Client: Yes, but only if I don't have anything on my mind!

Counselor: So, let's go back to the original question. If a miracle had happened overnight and you woke up, what would you be thinking?

Client: Nothing. I would be just thinking about what I am doing. I would wake up and feel calm. I would just enjoy lying in the coziness of my bed. Cuddling my husband. Feeling excited about my day.

Counselor: What would your husband notice about you?

Client: He would notice that I was just cuddling up to him. Not desperate to jump up like a cat on hot bricks.

Counselor: What would your husband notice about you as the day goes on?

Client: I would be like the old me. I'd be fun. If it wasn't a work day, I would suggest a walk in the park and maybe some lunch out somewhere.

Counselor: What would you be thinking about before you went out?

Client: I would be thinking about the lovely food I would be eating. I would be thinking about the nice walk in the forest I would be about to have.

Counselor: What else?

Client: I'd probably go online and have a look at their menu. Start thinking about what I wanted to eat! I used to do that all the time. I am pretty obsessive about food. Always thinking about my next meal and looking forward to it!

Counselor: What else would you be thinking?

Client: Usual stuff. What should I wear? How should I wear my hair, up or down?

Counselor: What would you be doing before going out?

Client: I'd be getting ready. Doing my make-up, getting my hair sorted, dressing myself!

Counselor: And what would you be thinking about while getting ready?

Client: I'd just be focusing on that really. I would be concentrating on putting my make up on. Thinking about what to wear. I would probably be wondering if there was anywhere else we could go after lunch. Maybe persuade Rob to do a bit of shopping in town. I'd then think through what I wanted to buy. What was missing from my wardrobe! I love getting new clothes.

(Clarifying what the client might be thinking about if the problem was not there can help her to think positively if the problem does not occur. I have found that just thinking this through can make clients more conscious of their thoughts. This often has the impact of the client consciously choosing to focus on these positive thoughts when next in that situation.)

Counselor: So, you would be concentrating on getting ready, you would be thinking about the day ahead and what you would like to do.

Client: Yes.

Counselor: On a scale of 0 to 10, 0 being nothing like your miracle day and 10 being your miracle day, where are you on the scale at the moment?

Client: 3.

Counselor: What would it look like at a 4?

Client: I would feel a bit calmer. I would be focusing on what I am doing a little more. Maybe my thoughts would focus more on what I am doing or about to do rather than focusing on the anxiety.

Counselor: How would you do that?

Client: I would consciously try to focus on what I am doing. I would try and distract myself. I don't think it would be enough to let me feel able to go outside though.

Counselor: What number on the scale would you need to be at before you felt that you were able to go outside?

Client: 5 or a 6.

Counselor: What would be happening at a 5 or 6?

Client: I would be thinking normal everyday thoughts a lot more.

Counselor: How would this help you feel like you could go outside?

Client: I'd feel calmer as I wouldn't be thinking about the anxiety so much.

Counselor: So, how can we get you to think more normal everyday thoughts?

Client: Maybe I could have a plan? A plan that I stick to. Of things that I could do or think about to distract me before I go out?

Counselor: I think that could really help you. What types of things could we put in your plan?

Client: Painting my nails springs to mind. I like to paint my nails. It makes me feel calm. I guess that's because I am concentrating on what I am doing.

Counselor: So before you go out, you could paint your nails. What else could we put in the plan?

Client: Maybe read my book? But sometimes my mind drifts when I read and I feel anxious. Perhaps that's not a good idea.

Counselor: Okay, what else could distract you?

Client: Ah! Phoning a friend! I said that earlier didn't I? That phoning a friend distracts me. I could phone a friend or mum or dad.

Counselor: Great. So you could paint your nails, phone someone, what else?

Client: Do some gentle housework. Like putting the clothes away. I think as long as I don't just sit in front of the TV waiting to go out it's got to help, hasn't it? At the moment, before I go out I watch TV but I just sit there and wait and get more and more anxious. I'll try this.

Counselor: How ready to you feel to try this, on a scale of 0 to 10, 0 being not at all ready and 10 being completely ready?

Client: About a 6.

Counselor: Is that enough for you to try?

(It's important to clarify whether the client is ready to make the step. If not, I have to find out what would help her feel ready to take that step or to try and find a different activity that she does feel ready to do.)

Client: Yes. I think so.

Counselor: Well, we are coming towards the end of our session now. So if it's okay with you I would just like to read my notes and then summarize the session.

(Summarizing the session is vital. During a session the client is having to think pretty hard. A lot of ground can be covered and it can be difficult to remember everything. The feedback helps to summarize the main points so they remain fresh in the clients mind. It is also used to agree the next steps.)

Client: Yes fine.

Counselor looks through notes.

Counselor: Thanks for being patient and waiting for me to look through my notes of our session.

Client: That's okay.

Counselor: I'd firstly like to say how much I appreciated your motivation and determination to overcome your difficulties. You really want to get better and are highly motivated to keep trying and persevering. You have already tried various strategies to try and manage your anxiety. You have found that distracting yourself can help you sometimes. When you are out you find that talking to someone nearby can help or looking at your phone. You sometimes send texts, look at Facebook or read the news. You also find calling a friend or family member can help too. I was really impressed that you came up with the idea of having a plan of distractions before you go out. These included nail painting, gentle housework or phoning a friend. I wonder if you think it might be helpful to play scrabble before you go out too, as you mentioned this helped to distract you a lot?

Client: Yes, I like that idea. Scrabble does keep my mind off things.

Counselor: Great. During the session I was also really impressed when you told me about how last week you felt calm and you took the opportunity to spontaneously go out for a walk around the block. You mentioned that going out when you feel calm is easier for you as you don't have to sit and worry about going out. I think it is really great that you recognize this.

(I'm clarifying what has impressed me. When someone is praised they are more likely to keep repeating that behavior. This statement is also highlighting what has worked for the client in the last week or so.)

Client: Thanks.

Counselor: Have you found today's session useful and would you like to come again?

Client: Yes, it has been useful. It has helped me to clarify what I find helpful. Hearing you say it all back to me has made me think maybe I should go out more often when I do feel calm. Perhaps if I can go out spontaneously when I feel calm, I will feel calmer going out when it is planned. It's almost like practicing going out when I am feeling at my best. What do you think?

Counselor: I think that's a great idea. I'm glad you have found today's session useful. Would you like to meet again and if so when?

Client: Yes, I'd like to meet again. Are you okay to come to me next week, same time and day?

Counselor: Let me check my diary.

Pause.

Counselor: Yes that's fine with me.

Client: Great.

Counselor: Between now and the next session I would like you to make a note of the times that you feel you are noticing a positive change.

Client: Okay, will do.

Counseling session ends.

Session Two

Counselor: Hi

Client: Hi

Counselor: How are you?

Client: Fine thanks. Come in.

Counselor and client sit down in lounge.

Counselor: How has your week been?

Client: Good actually. Really good.

Counselor: Oh yes?

Client: Yes. I was thinking about what we spoke about in the last session, you know, about going out spontaneously if I felt calm?

Counselor: Yes, I remember.

Client: And I did. I did just that. One evening we were just watching TV and I noticed that I was feeling calm. So I said to Rob, 'let's go for a walk'. We went for a walk around the block and when we were nearly home, I realized that actually I was feeling okay and could perhaps walk a little longer. So I suggested we carried on walking for a bit. Rob's face was a picture! I don't think he could believe it.

Counselor: That's great. How did you decide to do that?

Client: I just thought about what you said about doing things when I felt calm. I felt calm so I kept going.

Counselor: I am really impressed that you set yourself a goal and then recognized that you could do more than your original goal and carried on.

Client: It felt great. Just being able to be out of the house for more than 20 minutes. It was great.

Counselor: Did you know you could do that?

Client: No! I didn't think I would be able to do that. I still can't believe that I did it!

Counselor: What have you learned from this achievement?

Client: That I can go out. It helps to not have things planned. To just do them, for now. I mean once I get used to going out again, maybe I can start planning to go out.

(I want to drill down into the client's thinking patterns. I want to know what positive thoughts helped the client and if she could use these again.)

Counselor: What were you saying to yourself when you were walking around the block?

Client: I was thinking...I was thinking and feeling that I can do this. I'm okay. I don't feel too bad at all.

Counselor: During the walk around the block how did you feel?

Client: I felt calm. There were moments when I could feel a little bit of anxiety rising in me but they disappeared and I was fine. They were like little spikes of anxiety but only small ones that didn't bother me too much. There were only small. They were bearable.

Counselor: So, during the walk you felt small spikes of anxiety which you were able to tolerate and the anxiety faded away.

Client: Yes.

Counselor: How did you manage to overcome the small levels of anxiety? What did you say to yourself?

Client: Oh, I don't know. Let me think.

Silence.

Client: I'm just trying to think back to that night.

Counselor: Okay. What were your thoughts?

Client: That it was only anxiety. I'd be okay.

Counselor: So you said to yourself 'it's only anxiety, I'll be okay'.

Client: Yes. I know that the anxiety can't harm me. I know that nothing will happen to me and that night I believed it. But I think it was because the anxiety was only mild. It wasn't like I was having a panic attack.

Counselor: Still, you managed to overcome your anxiety and feel calm once again. That's a big achievement.

Client: You think so?

Counselor: Yes, definitely.

Client: Great.

Counselor: Going back to that walk around the block you said to yourself that it is only anxiety. I'll be okay. What else did you think?

Client: It'll pass. It can't harm me. I'll be okay. And me and Rob were talking about decorating the bedroom which was keeping my mind occupied as I was imaging the colors and the soft furnishings and all of that. And I was feeling excited about it. Looking forward to getting rid of the awful wallpaper we have in that room at the moment. It's really dated and I don't really like being in there at the moment.

Counselor: How could you use what you have learned from this achievement?

Client: What do you mean?

Counselor: Knowing how you overcame the anxiety during the walk around the block, how could you use this knowledge to overcome anxiety in other situations?

Client: I guess to tell myself that it is only anxiety and it can't harm me. To tell myself that if I distract myself, it will pass. It's when I think about it, that it doesn't help. When I think about the anxiety and imagine myself fainting or being sick, then I start to panic and have a massive panic attack and don't want to go out ever again.

Counselor: Visualizing yourself fainting or being sick results in increased panic.

Client: Yes.

Counselor: What were you visualizing when you were on the walk the other night?

(I want the client to realize what visualizations help her to feel calm. Knowing what not to focus on can help but having something else to focus on instead can further increase the chances of success.)

Client: I was thinking about myself being okay.

Counselor: What pictures were running through your mind?

Client: Just of myself further on the walk and being okay.

Counselor: So rather than picturing yourself fainting or being sick, you were picturing yourself being okay a little further along in your journey?

Client: Yes, yes I was.

Counselor: How could you apply this to other situations when you feel anxious?

Client: I could picture myself at a point in the near future where I am feeling okay. So, if I went to the local shop, I could try picturing myself walking home and feeling calm. Or standing at the till feeling calm. Oh but

I can't do it. It's not going to work. I can't go to the shop. It's not enough to make me feel okay about that.

Counselor: What situation would it be okay to try it in?

Client: Don't know. Something really small. Like walking to the end of the road and back. On my own.

Counselor: On a scale of 0 to 10, 0 being you don't feel ready to try and 10 being you feel ready to try walking to the end of the road and back. Where on the scale are you today?

Client: I don't know. Maybe a 6.

Counselor: Is a 6 enough for you to walk out of the door and try it?

Client: Yea, I guess so. But it's such a small thing. It's almost, like, what's the point. If I do it, it's not like I've made it to the shops or anything is it? All I have done is walk to the end of the road and back.

Counselor: So you feel that the task is too easy?

Client: Yea kind of!

Counselor: How would you feel about doing it now?

Client: What? Right now?

Counselor: Yes.

Client: What and you would stay here and wait for me?

Counselor: Yes.

Client: Yea. I reckon I could do it. Shall I do it? Really?

Counselor: Would you like to?

Client: Yea, okay. Why not! I'll just get my shoes on. It's not far, I should only be about 5 minutes max.

Counselor: Okay. I'll wait.

Client: I'll take my phone with me.

Counselor: Okay.

Client leaves the house and returns about 4 minutes later.

Client: Hi! I did it!

Counselor: Great! How do you feel?

Client: I feel amazing! Do you know how nice it felt to be out on my own? Even though it was for a short while. It felt great! It's a beautiful day out there too. Really nice to just feel like I was out. It made a nice change.

Counselor: How do you think Rob will react when you tell him you've been out today?

Client: I'm not sure he'll be that impressed that I walked to the end of the road and back. I think I would need to do more to impress him.

Counselor: How do you feel about your achievement?

Client: Great. I know it was only a small walk but actually I feel like I really achieved something there. Even though it was small it makes me think I can do this.

Counselor: What have you learned from this?

Client: That even doing something small like walking to the end of the road and back can help.

Counselor: How could you apply what you have learned? What have you learned today that could help you towards to your goal of feeling calmer when you go out?

(I want the client to keep recognizing what she has learned from doing an activity. It's all about finding out what helps her to feel calm and overcome the anxiety).

Client: Maybe I could try really small steps. Like really small steps. So each time I try something it is just a tiny bit more difficult than what I tried to do before.

Counselor: Can you give me an example?

Client: Yes, like say the next time I go out I walk another 10 steps or something. Or 20. No that feels too much. An extra 10 steps. That feels like it would be easy.

Counselor: So you could try making small steps that feel easy to you.

Client: Yea. Like walking to the end of the road and back felt easy. Adding an extra 10 steps feels easy. Then maybe the next time I could make it a bit further and so on. Just keep doing it and going out lots and making lots of small trips each one just a tiny bit further. Yes I like that idea. That might work. Oh, but just thinking of adding all those trips together and eventually walking round the block feels too hard.

Counselor: So walking round the block on your own feels too difficult at the moment but the small step of walking to the end of the road plus 10 steps feels okay?

Client: Yes.

Counselor: To summarize then, you will try doing tasks that feel easy to you. How does walking to the end of the road plus 10 steps feel to you now?

Client: Easy.

Counselor: What obstacles might arise that may prevent you from doing this?

(I want the client to be aware of the obstacles. That way we can pre-think them and have a plan in place to deal with them.)

Client: Hmm... The only obstacles that might arise would be in my mind.

Counselor: Okay.

Client: Like, I might get to the point where I can't take the next small step. That actually it feels like it's too larger step.

Counselor: What would you do in that situation?

Client: Hmm... I don't know.

Counselor: What options would you have? If you didn't feel ready to progress to the next small step you had in your mind, what could you try instead?

Client: Err...I don't know.

Silence.

Client: Maybe...maybe I could just keep doing the step I'm on.

Counselor: Can you explain that to me?

Client: Yes, what about if I just keep doing what I was already doing. Keep doing it until I felt comfortable to go further?

Counselor: Yes, that could work.

Client: So, let's say I get to the post box. And I've done that. I've made it to the post box. But the thought of the post box plus 10 steps is too much. I feel anxious about it and can't picture myself doing it. So instead I just keep making it to the post box. I keep walking to the post box and maybe I have to do it 10 times or something. But after doing it 10 times maybe it will feel normal and I can then try walking the extra 10 steps. Maybe by that point walking to the post box will feel normal and I will feel that walking the extra 10 steps will be easy.

Counselor: How will you know that you are ready to try the next step?

Client: Because it will feel easy. I would feel like I did today, that I can do it. That it is within my capabilities. Maybe that's where I've gone wrong in the past. I've tried to jump too bigger step and then failed. It knocks my confidence when I can't do something.

Counselor: So rather than taking large steps that you don't feel ready for, you could try smaller steps that you do feel ready for.

Client: Yes. I'm just thinking too that maybe if I don't feel ready to make the next 10 steps when I go out for a walk, maybe I could take one step. I can always do one extra step can't I?

Counselor: Yes.

Client: No, actually that doesn't sit well. Just adding one step at a time. I think I would feel more comfortable to just keep doing the same step over and over until I feel comfortable moving forward to the next step.

Counselor: I think it's really good that you are able to identify when a goal feels comfortable to you and when it does not. It's good that you can anticipate what you will feel about a goal in the future.

Client: Yea, it might change when I get to that point. But for now I think I would like to think of my goal as just keep repeating the same task or activity or whatever I should call it, until I feel completely ready to take the next step.

Counselor: So if 0 is not ready at all and 10 is completely ready, where do you think you will need to be on the scale before attempting the next small step?

Client: A 6 probably. Like today. I was a 6 today.

Counselor: So when you feel like you are a 6 on the scale, that is high enough for you to feel ready to move on to the next step.

Client: Yes. I'll feel a little anxious and feel like it's a challenge but it will be a challenge that I can cope with. It will be a small level of anxiety that I can tolerate. It will feel easy. Well not 'easy, easy' but easy-ish to do. I'll feel capable of doing it. I think that is what I am trying to say.

Counselor: How will you decide what your next small step is?

Client: Um...I don't know. I think I'll just know what my next step is. At that time I'll know what I feel comfortable with. So for now, I know that my next step will be to walk to the end of the road and then an extra 10 steps. Today that feels 'easy' to me.

Counselor: What else do you know about feeling calmer when you go out that could help you with your next step?

Client: To not plan it! For now anyway at least. I'll just go out at some point in the day when I feel able to. I can't plan it, not just yet.

Counselor: Is that something you would like to think about today too? About planning to go out?

Client: No. Not really. If that's okay with you? I like that I have managed to go out twice spontaneously. I don't want to ruin it by planning to do something and then not being able to do it. Is that okay with you?

Counselor: Of course. I think it's good that you are recognizing what you feel able and not able to do just yet. When will you know that you are ready to start planning to go out?

Client: Huh! I don't know! Maybe when I can walk to the shop on my own, maybe then.

Counselor: Okay. Is today's session helping so far?

Client: Yes, it's helping to get it straight in my mind what my next steps are. It feels good to have a plan.

Counselor: Are we talking about what you want to talk about. Is there anything we should be addressing today?

(I want to make sure that we are talking about what the client wants to talk about. If I didn't check I might find she raises important issues at the

end of the session which can then be difficult to deal with in the allocated time.)

Client: No, not really. I can't think of anything. I think it would be helpful to talk about actually managing a panic attack. So if I do have one I know what to do.

Counselor: What have you tried to do in the past to manage a panic attack? What has helped? What has not helped?

Client: Nothing seems to help. When I have a panic attack, I just feel awful. I go all hot and sweaty. I can feel my top lip actually starts to sweat. It sounds gross, doesn't it? I feel sick like I am actually on the verge of being sick. You know when you are about to be sick and you get those few moments beforehand when you are like 'I'm going to throw up' and you just know that you are going to throw up, like, for sure?

Counselor: Yes.

Client: It feels like that. It feels like I am about to throw up and I picture myself throwing up wherever I am. So if I was in the supermarket, I would picture myself throwing up in the supermarket aisle. It's just awful. And I feel dizzy. Like really light-headed. I feel like I am going to faint. Just pass out there and then. Oh and I can't breathe. I just need to get out of wherever I am. I just need to breathe fresh air.

Counselor: So breathing fresh air helps.

Client: Yes. Wherever I am I have to escape as quick as I can.

Counselor: What do you know about panic attacks that could help you manage them?

Client: Well, um...I'm not sure. I guess I know that they pass.

Counselor: What else do you know about them?

Client: It's something to do with the adrenalin in the body. It's fight or flight or something like that.

Counselor: What else?

Client: They can't actually harm you. It's something to do with when we were cavemen and we had the choice to fight the animal or run away. But in today's modern society it doesn't really matter. We don't really need it but it's still there and it can manifest itself in panic attacks.

Counselor: Yes, so it's the body's way of reacting to a perceived threat. You said that panic attacks pass?

Client: Yes, they do.

Counselor: How long does it take for your panic attack to pass?

Client: Oh I don't know. It depends.

Counselor: On what?

Client: On what I am thinking about I guess. If I engage with it, it will get worse or carry on. Then it can last for... oh I don't know really. I suppose in actual fact the real intense panic attack only lasts, what, maybe a couple of minutes.

Counselor: Then what happens?

Client: Then I still feel anxious, really anxious but it's not a panic attack. It's just anxiety. But if I hang around I will have another panic attack.

Counselor: Where on the scale, 0 being not very bad at all and 10 being really bad, is the severity of the first panic attack you usually experience?

Client: Oh, I don't know. Maybe an 8 sometimes a 9.

Counselor: If you do stay in the situation and experience another panic attack where on the scale is the level of severity? 0 being not very bad at all and 10 being really bad?

Client: Hmm... That's interesting. I want to say it's a little less. I think the first one is always the worst. That's the killer! I usually flee at that point.

Counselor: Where would you place it on the scale, the second panic attack? If you had to give it a severity rating?

Client: Probably a 7 1/2 .

Counselor: So the panic attacks get less severe.

(I am working with the client to help her clarify the 'truths' about how she experiences panic attacks. It can be easy to generalize all panic attacks. Asking questions about them can help to identify exceptions and rewrite the 'truths'.)

Client: Yes, I think they do. I don't really know. But I think they might.

Counselor: You said that you usually flee when you have a panic attack. On the occasions that you stay, what helps you to stay in the situation?

Client: Usually when I can't get out of it. When I have no choice. Like if I was on a bus or something like that. I don't tend to put myself in situations where I experience panic attacks. I tend to avoid them. I haven't, for example, been on a bus in years.

Counselor: So when you were in a situation where you were having a panic attack and you had no choice but to stay in the situation, how did you cope?

Client: I don't know. Some of these questions are really difficult! They are making me really have to think! What helped me to cope? I guess I didn't have any choice but to cope.

Counselor: In that situation, you still coped. You didn't have a choice but you still managed to cope.

Client: It doesn't really count though does it? I didn't wittingly stay and cope with it. I didn't decide to stay and face it. I would have run away if I could.

Counselor: Maybe. But ultimately you still coped with the panic attack. You still managed it. You still stayed in the situation.

Client: Yea. I suppose I did.

Counselor: How did you manage to cope? What helped?

Client: I don't think I did anything really. I just sat there, had the panic attack and then it passed.

Counselor: So, you were sitting down and the panic attack came and then it went?

Client: Yes.

Counselor: What does this tell us about panic attacks?

Client: That they come and go. Oh and that they only last a few minutes.

Counselor: Can we use this information to help us in anyway?

Client: Hmm... I don't know. Even knowing they only last a few minutes doesn't take away the fact that they are terrifying and I want to avoid them.

Counselor: How are you feeling before you experience a panic attack?

Client: Anxious.

Counselor: What are the final thoughts that run through your mind before a panic attack happens?

Client: That I am going to pass out or that I am going to be sick. I'd be feeling anxious and then I would feel that I was going to pass out or be sick. Actually I would probably imagine myself being sick or passing out wherever I am. Then the panic attack would come.

Counselor: Is there anything you have learned about managing your anxiety when it is of a lower level that could help us here? Is there anything that you learned from your walk around the block that could prove useful in this situation?

Client: I'm not sure. I can't remember what we said now!

Counselor: Let me consult my notes.

Pause.

Counselor: Right, one thing you said was that it helped to picture yourself at a point in the near future when you were feeling okay. So in relation to the walk around the block you pictured yourself a little further along the walk and feeling okay.

Client: So how could I apply that to a panic attack?

Counselor: What do we know? We know that your immediate thoughts before a panic attack are imagining yourself being sick or fainting. We know...

Client: Ah! So maybe if I could replace my thoughts with imagining myself a few minutes in the future and feeling calmer, the panic attacks wouldn't happen? Instead of imaging myself being sick or fainting, I could try to picture myself feeling calmer and acting normally in whatever situation I was in.

Counselor: I think that's a great idea. What else do we know about panic attacks that could help us?

Client: That they only last a few minutes. That they pass.

Counselor: How could that help you during a panic attack?

Client: I could remind myself that they don't last forever. And the next one might be less powerful.

Counselor: Yes. What else could you try to manage a panic attack?

Client: To breathe deeply but that doesn't help. If anything it makes me feel more light-headed.

Counselor: Do you know of any other strategies you could use?

Client: No, not really.

Counselor: Do you know of anyone else who has had panic attacks and overcome them?

Client: Yes. My mum used to have them.

Counselor: Do you know what she did to overcome them? How did she manage them?

Client: I don't know. I could ask her. I know that she always says 'you can't let them beat you'.

Counselor: So determination runs in the family!

Client: Yes! I guess it does!

Counselor: How are you feeling today's session is progressing?

Client: Yea, good. Having a plan, a strategy, in place is helping. It's making me feel like I know what I need to do.

Counselor: What would you like to see happen between now and your next session? What are your best hopes?

Client: I would like to be able to say to you next time that I have walked to the end of the road plus 10 steps. I think that would be a step in the right direction.

Counselor: If you managed to do that, what difference would that make to you?

Client: Oh, I would be so pleased. I would feel like I was really starting to make a bit of progress. I know that it's only small steps but I can build on these. Once I get my strategies in place I can start moving forward. Slowly and steadily at a pace that I feel is comfortable. Not doing too much. I don't want to freak myself out and fail all over again.

Counselor: What do you think Rob's response will be when he sees that you are starting to take small steps and starting to go out again?

(Asking about another important person's response can help to further increase the client's motivation.)

Client: He will be over the moon. It will show him that I am serious about getting better. It will show him that I am making the effort and that I can get better. I hope that he will see that I'm getting better and this will make him feel less inclined to leave me. I know it sounds silly. He is my husband after all, in sickness and in health and all that, but it does worry me. I worry that he will leave me.

Counselor: You're concerned he may leave you?

Client: Yes. I don't think he will but if I could start showing him that I am getting better that's got to help. It will give him hope too.

Counselor: If Rob noticed that you were getting better, what difference would that make to you?

Client: I would feel so much better. It would make me feel a bit more secure in our relationship.

Counselor: Okay. We are coming towards the end of our session now. As before, I would like to take a few moments to look through my notes to summarize the session for us and agree what is going to happen next. Is that okay with you?

Client: Yes of course.

Counselor looks through notes.

Counselor: I'd firstly like to say how much I appreciated your honesty in today's session. If the goals we were planning didn't feel comfortable to you, you let me know straight away. I also thought it was great how you were able to predict what would and would not feel comfortable in the future. I was impressed with how you thought of a way to manage this. For example, you mentioned that if you didn't feel comfortable taking the next small step you would keep repeating the same step until you did feel comfortable taking the next step.

Client: Thanks

Counselor: I was also really impressed that you walked to the end of the road and back today. You felt that it would be easy to do and you took the opportunity to just do it. I was also really impressed that since the last session you managed to walk around the block with Rob. I think it was great that you noticed that you still felt calm at the end of the walk and decided to walk a little further.

To summarize today's session, we spoke about doing small steps that felt easy to you. You mentioned that your next small step would be to walk to the end of the road and back, plus 10 steps. We spoke about various things that would help you on the walk such as picturing yourself a little further ahead and feeling calm. We talked about how anxiety comes and goes. You mentioned that if you tell yourself that it is only anxiety and it will pass, it can help you to feel calm. You also mentioned that if you can distract yourself and think about something else this can also help you to feel calm.

We spoke about panic attacks and we wondered if the second panic attack was less severe than the first panic attack. You mentioned that your panic attacks only last a few minutes and visualizing yourself being okay in the very near future may help to prevent the panic attack occurring in the first place. You said that your mum had overcome panic attacks and you might ask how she managed to do this.

Client: Yep. We've covered quite a lot today!

Counselor: We have. Have you found today's sessions useful?

Client: Yes very. It makes me feel like I want to get out there today and try my next step!

Counselor: That's great! I really admire your motivation! Would you like to have another session?

(It's up to the client whether they have another session or not. It is also up to the client when they wish to come again. The idea is that the client knows better than the counselor how they feel and when would be the best time to see the counselor again.)

Client: Yes please. Could I have one next week?

Counselor: Of course. Same time, same day?

Client: Yes please.

Counselor: Right, you are all booked in. In between today and our next session, I would like you to notice once again any positive changes. Try to make a note of them and what you were thinking about at the time.

(I want the client to keep noticing positive changes. These positive changes can hold possible solutions.)

Client: Okay. I'll jot them down.

Counselor: Great. Right then, I'll see you next week.

Client: Thanks. Thanks very much.

Counseling session ends.

Session Three

Counselor: Hi

Client: Hi, come in.

Counselor: Thanks. How are you today?

Client: Not great to be honest.

Counselor: Oh dear.

Client: Please take a seat.

Counselor: Thanks.

Both counselor and client down in the lounge.

Counselor: So what's been happening?

Client: Oh, I've had a terrible week. Awful. I've really let myself down.

Counselor: Do you want to tell me about it?

(The client doesn't need to tell me about it if they don't want to or they don't feel ready to.)

Client: Yea, I probably should.

Counselor: You don't have to if you don't want to.

Client: No, I want to. I think it might help.

Counselor: Okay.

Client: Well, I went out for a walk with Rob and I thought I would be okay. It was spontaneous. I decided to go at the last minute. Well, on the walk I started to feel anxious. I was really annoyed at myself for feeling anxious. I had been doing so well and this made me realize how far I've got to go or rather how far from feeling well I actually am. Anyway, I had this massive panic attack. I just couldn't help it. I started panicking and just wanted to get home. Rob gave me a hug and tried to encourage me to carry on but I just wanted to go home. He kept pushing me to keep walking. Telling me that I would be okay. But I knew I wouldn't be. I just wanted to go home.

Well, he lost his patience a bit and started shouting at me. Saying that he couldn't understand me. He couldn't understand what I was scared of. He said 'but you are never sick and you don't ever faint. I just don't understand what the problem is.' He just kept on and on all the while I'm panicking and he's not moving. He's just standing there while I am desperate to go back home. Usually he is so good but this time he was just being an idiot. That's unfair. I know he was trying to help. So I beg him, literally beg him, to walk with me back home. But he refuses! Can you believe that? He actually point blank refuses. He says,' I'm going round the block'. You can either walk back home on your own or you can come round the block with me. I couldn't believe it!

Counselor: What did you do?

Client: I had no choice really. I couldn't walk back home on my own. I had to go with him. It was awful. The whole way round the block I was just crying and we were arguing about it. I don't know what was wrong with him, he is usually so good about stuff like this but it was weird. It was like he was trying to give me 'tough love'. But it's just made me frightened. I don't feel like I can go out with him again. It's frightened me and I don't feel safe going out with him again. What if he does it again? What if he won't take me home? Knowing that he might behave that way again and not take me home makes me feel really anxious. I can't imagine being able to go out with him again. And where does that leave us?

Counselor: It sounds like you've had a difficult time.

Client: It just really shook me up. I feel like I'm back to square one. Worse than square one. If I hadn't tried to go out, then I wouldn't be in this position. I really don't know what to do. I wonder if we are going to split up.

Counselor: How have things been since that walk?

Client: Alright. We've spoken about it since but he stands by what he did. He said that he couldn't believe that I was doing this to us. Like I actually have a choice! If I had a choice, does he not think that I would choose to be well? It's not like I am putting it on for fun, is it? I wonder if someone has said to him to give me tough love and I'll just snap out of it or something along those lines. It wouldn't surprise me. I just don't know how we go forward from here.

Counselor: Okay.

Client: And worse than that I've been anxious all week. I haven't been able to go out on my own either. I have been stuck in this house and it's doing my head in. If I can't go out on my own and I can't go out with Rob, how am I ever supposed to get better? How am I ever going to get over this?

Counselor: Is there anyone else you feel could help you?

Client: My mum, I suppose. I could go out with my mum.

Counselor: Anyone else?

Client: Yes, my friends maybe. No, actually I don't think my friends would understand.

Counselor: Would any of your friends understand and be able to help you?

Client: Yea, maybe one actually. My friend Jo would be great at helping me. I'd feel safe with her.

Counselor: So, you could go out with your mum or with your friend Jo.

Client: Yep.

Counselor: I know it's been a tough week.

Client: Yep, it's been pretty dire.

Counselor: How did you cope?

Client: I just told myself that once I get better none of this will matter. I know it's not Rob's fault that he doesn't understand. I'm not sure I would if I was in his position. But he just doesn't listen. It's like he is quiet but he doesn't actually listen. It doesn't sink in.

Counselor: It can be difficult for other people to understand anxiety. So you told yourself that once you get better none of this will matter. What do we know about you that reassures us that you will get better?

Client: That I'm determined.

Counselor: So, how was the rest of the week?

Client: Awful. I just couldn't do it. It was too hard. I couldn't do any of it.

(I want to find the exceptions in the client's week. There are probably some days or times that were better than others. We can learn from those times.)

Counselor: Were there some days that were better than others?

Client: Nope. They were all terrible.

(Clients often remember the times most recent to them, usually the past few days. This can over shadow any successes they had earlier on the week. By asking various questions I am hoping to discover the better times. This will help the client to adopt a more rational frame of mind when thinking about the last week and provide us with some positive successes to talk about.)

Counselor: So, we saw each other last Wednesday afternoon.

Client: Yep.

Counselor: How was Thursday?

Client: Thursday was okay. Actually, on Wednesday when you left, I walked to the end of the road again and I did my plus 10 steps.

Counselor: That's great. What made you decide to that?

Client: I felt really boosted after our last session. I decided that I wanted to try. I felt full of confidence. It feels such a long time ago now. So much has happened in a week.

Counselor: It has been a difficult week.

Client: Hasn't it just? I wish I could just erase last week. Go back to feeling like I did when you left the other week.

Counselor: What did you feel when I left last week?

Client: I felt confident. Full of hope. Look where that got me.

Counselor: What would it take to get you back to feeling confident and full of hope again?

Client: A miracle!

Counselor: How do you feel about the strategies we came up with during the last session?

Client: I think they can still work. I think that I just need to get my confidence back.

Counselor: What helped you to feel confident at the end of the last session?

Client: I think the fact that I had gone for the walk on my own helped me a lot. It gave me a confidence boost. Made me realize that I could do it. That I could go out on my own. Even if just for a short while.

Counselor: How do we get that confidence back?

Client: Go for another walk?

Counselor: Okay. On a scale of 0 to 10, 0 being not confident and 10 being very confident, how confident do you feel about going for a walk in a few minutes?

Client: About a 5.

Counselor: A 5. That's good. What is making you a 5 and not a 0?

Client: Because I've done it before, I know I can do it again. It's just that panic attack from before. It's made me feel less sure of myself.

Counselor: What would make you feel more sure of yourself?

Client: Just doing the walk I guess. If I did that, I think it would build my confidence and then each time I did something my confidence would grow some more.

Counselor: So your confidence would come back the more times you go out?

Client: Yes. Over time I would forget about the panic attack and it wouldn't bother me so much.

Counselor: You mentioned you were a 5 on the scale when we spoke about you going for a walk.

Client: Yes.

Counselor: Is that high enough for you to go out?

Client: I'm not sure. It's on the edge.

Counselor: What would get you to a 6?

Client: I'm not sure.

Counselor: What can we do to make you feel a little bit more confident about walking to the end of the road and back?

Client: I don't know.

Counselor: What would help?

Client: Ah! I can't think of anything.

Silence.

Client: Maybe if you wait for me at the end of drive? Or if you have your phone on you and I can call you if I feel bad and you can walk to meet me?

Counselor: We can do that. Which would you prefer?

Client: If I take my phone with me and ring you.

Counselor: Okay. How do you feel about walking to the end of the road and back now?

Client: Still a 5, but I think that's okay. Knowing I can contact you helps. Maybe I can do this. All I can do is try, isn't it? I really don't want to fail though.

Counselor: Even if you come home before you make it to the end of the road and back, it's still progress.

Client: Is it?

Counselor: I think so. If you make it 10 steps outside, that's better than you staying here and making no steps outside.

Client: Yes, I suppose so.

(The client isn't entirely comfortable about walking to the end of the road and back. She isn't feeling confident that it is within her capabilities. I want to remind her of our previous discussion about small steps and see if she thinks this may help her now.)

Counselor: In the last session we spoke about doing small steps that felt easy. What would feel an easy goal to you right now?

Client: Walking half way up the road and back.

Counselor: On the scale, of 0 to 10, 0 being very difficult and 10 being easy, where would walking half way up the road and back be?

Client: About an 8.

Counselor: So that would be a fairly easy task for you.

Client: Yes, but isn't that going backwards? It's less than what I did last week.

(It is less than last week but I feel it would still be progress. It would still be better than doing nothing. I need to check whether that is how the client would feel too so I use scaling questions.)

Counselor: How do you feel about where you are right now? On the scale of 0 to 10, 0 being nowhere near your ideal future of feeling calmer when out and 10 being feeling calmer when out, where are you on the scale right now?

Client: About a 2.

Counselor: If you were to walk half way up the road and back, where do you think you might feel you are on the scale then?

Client: About a 2 and a half.

Counselor: So by walking half way up the road and back, which you feel would be easy to do, you would move half a point on the scale.

Client: Yes

Counselor: Well...

Client: So I might as well do it and move half a point up the scale. Better than where I am right now?

Counselor: Do you think?

Client: Yes. Okay. Let's do that. I'll try walking half way up the road and back again.

Counselor: Okay.

Client: See you in a bit then!

Client returns.

Counselor: How did you get on?

Client: Yea, alright actually. I felt okay. I even went to nearly the end of the road.

Counselor: Excellent. What made you decide to do that?

Client: I felt okay when I got halfway and thought actually I can go a bit further.

Counselor: So when you achieved your initial goal and still felt calm, you were okay to continue. You were able to add on another small step.

Client: Yes! It's the same thing as before isn't it. Try a small step and then if I feel okay carry on for as long as I want to.

Counselor: Yes. So if I ask you the same question again now, if 0 on the scale is not feeling calm when you are outside and 10 on the scale is feeling calmer when you are outside where are you now on the scale?

Client: About a 4.

Counselor: Excellent. So you have just moved up from a 2 to a 4. What has helped you do that?

Client: You.

(It's important that the client owns all the solutions as her own. I want the client to know that she has the answers within her.)

Counselor: No, I only asked the questions. You came up with all the answers.

Client: Okay, then. Me!

Counselor: What helped you to move from a 2 to a 4? What have you learned from what's happened today?

Client: That if I fail, I can get back on the horse. If I fail, I need to think of a goal that I would feel is easy, something that felt easily within my grasp, within my capabilities. Something that I know I can do.

Counselor: And how does that help?

Client: It gets my confidence back. I can build it back up again quickly, the goals I mean. I might even be able to go beyond my initial goal if I feel okay when I'm out.

Counselor: Great.

Client: And if I have already done those goals, I imagine that I will be able to speed my way through them a lot quicker than the first time I did them.

Counselor: Great.

Client: I'm starting to feel a bit better now.

Counselor: Good. What's helped?

Client: Just talking it through and getting my head straight. Doing something constructive about it and having a plan back again. A 'failure' plan. I now have a failure plan!

Counselor: Yes, if you experience a setback in the future, you will have a plan already to go.

Client: It feels good.

Counselor: We are already a fair way into the session but is there anything in particular you would like to get out of today's session?

Client: Yes. I'd like to talk about how I managed, or didn't manage, to cope with the panic attack last week. I'd also like to talk about how to manage my husband! I would like to know what to say to him to make him understand.

Counselor: What do you feel would be the most helpful? Our original goal was to help you to feel calmer when outside. We can talk about your husband in as much as it helps with the original goal. It's important that we focus on one goal at a time.

(Focusing on more than goal would become confusing. The work would be diluted. It's important to work on one goal at a time.)

Client: I guess talking about how to manage the panic attack would help more. It would be the original goal and having less panic attacks and knowing how to manage them while out with my husband. It might stop the situation with my husband from arising again anyway.

Counselor: So you would like to talk more about managing the panic attacks?

Client: Yes.

Counselor: When you experienced the panic attack last week, what helped and what didn't help?

Client: I tried to do all the things we said but I couldn't remember them when I was having the panic attack. I was too busy panicking.

Counselor: How many panic attacks did you have?

Client: I don't know. Maybe three or four for the whole walk.

(I am hoping to investigate whether the panic attacks got less severe as the client suspected previously. This is a good opportunity to analyze the severity of the panic attacks and either prove or disprove the theory. If the panic attacks get less this could help the client's mindset a great deal.)

Counselor: How severe was the first panic attack on a scale of 0 to 10, 0 being not severe and 10 being very severe?

Client: About an 8 or a 9.

Counselor: How severe was the second panic attack on the scale? 0 being not severe and 10 being very severe?

Client: I don't know. Maybe about a 6. Or a 7.

Counselor: And the third?

Client: I can't really remember the third or fourth clearly. Perhaps a 5 or a 6?

Counselor: Can you remember the last panic attack?

Client: A bit. Maybe a 4. I was so angry at my husband by that point that I wasn't really concentrating on them anymore.

Counselor: So the first panic attack was fairly severe. The second panic attack was a little less. And the last few panic attacks were much less.

Client: Yes. They got less severe. They got easier to cope with. We wondered that, didn't we? And that certainly seems to be the case. Well for this occasion anyway.

Counselor: Yes, the first seems the worst and then they lessen.

Client: That's good to know.

Counselor: How will that information help you?

Client: Hmm... I guess I can tell myself when I am having the first one that the others will be less.

Counselor: How will that help you?

Client: Well because I can say to myself 'if I can just manage this one, the next will be less'. And if I keep going, they will get less and less.

Counselor: So when you are experiencing a panic attack, you can say to yourself that this panic attack is the worst and they will get less severe.

Client: Yes, I can say to myself that if they carry on, they will get less and less and I will feel okay. I'll be okay.

Counselor: Good.

Client: I know also that I am always alright. They don't harm me.

Counselor: Are there any occasions when you have said that to yourself when having a panic attack?

Client: Yes. But it doesn't work. It's like I know it but I don't know it. If you know what I mean. It's like I know that's the case but in my panic I don't quite believe it.

Counselor: On a scale of 0 to 10, 0 being you don't believe it at all and 10 being you completely believe it, where on the scale would you be during a panic attack if you told yourself that you will be okay?

Client: Probably about a 2 or maybe a 3.

Counselor: On the scale or 0 to 10, the same again, 0 being you don't believe it at all and 10 being you completely believe it, where on the scale, during a panic attack, would you be if you told yourself that the first panic attack is the worst and they will get less severe.

Client: Oh probably a 8 or a 9. That is unless I have a situation where my panic attacks get worse.

Counselor: What do you mean?

Client: Well, I might tell myself that and then actually my panic attacks get worse.

Counselor: Previously you thought your panic attacks got less and then during your walk last week you discovered they did get less.

Client: Yea I think they do get less. But that's why I am saying it's an 8 or a 9 and not a 10. I have a small bit of doubt.

Counselor: Ah okay. Makes sense. Was there anything else on that walk that happened that we could learn from? Did anything else help you to cope with the panic attacks?

Client: My anger! I was angry at Rob and that made me think about that rather than my fear.

Counselor: Do you think it was the anger that helped or the fact that you were thinking about something else other than your fear?

(I want to clarify what is actually helping here and whether it is something she could use in future when experiencing panic attacks.)

Client: Probably that I was thinking about something else other than the fear.

Counselor: So thinking of something else can help?

Client: Yes, it's the old distraction thing again isn't it? Keep my mind off things.

Counselor: So let's imagine that you have gone out for a walk. On this day you are able to manage your panic attacks. You have a small panic attack and you tell yourself that the panic attack will pass in a few minutes and the next one won't be so bad. You then distract yourself. How would you distract yourself? What would you think about?

Client: Oh. I don't know. Let me think.

Silence.

Client: I could think through how I want to decorate the rooms of my house that haven't been done yet.

Counselor: Great. What else?

Client: Umm... I could.....I could, oh it's quite tricky this. I don't know.

Counselor: Take your time. There is no rush.

Client: Maybe think through how I would like the garden.

Counselor: What else?

(I keep asking what else in order for the client to have plenty of things to think about should she experience another panic attack.)

Client: I could think about my guitar playing. Think about my chords and where I need to put my fingers.

Counselor: Okay. Anything else? What else could help distract you?

Client: Ah, call someone on my phone. Engage in a conversation. Like we said before.

Counselor: Great. So to summarize, if you had a panic attack when you were out, you would firstly tell yourself that it will only last a few minutes. You would then tell yourself that the next panic attack won't be as bad and so on. They will get less and less. Once the panic attack has passed you would distract yourself by thinking about how to decorate your home or garden or you would call someone on your phone.

Client: Yes. Sounds easy when you say it like that but it's much tougher in practice.

Counselor: On the scale 0 to 10, 0 being not confident at all and 10 being very confident, how confident do you feel about managing panic attacks when you are out?

Client: About a 4.

Counselor: Okay.

Client: I still feel scared of them. I guess I won't go any higher up the scale until I have had a panic attack and managed to cope with it. Until these ideas work. Then I will feel more confident.

Counselor: Is 4 high enough on the scale for you to try going out?

Client: Yea of course. I would probably feel okay trying to go out even if it was a 2. I'm scared of them and I don't think that's going to change overnight. I need to go out to try and learn to manage to cope with them. But it helps having a different strategy in my mind now. Something else to try. It makes me a feel a little bit more hopeful. Not much but a little bit. I keep thinking about the panic attacks coming for a few minutes and then going again. They are like contractions aren't they? Like something I just need to put up with for a few minutes until they pass. I've never had children but it's like contractions that get less and less rather than getting worse!

Counselor: So the panic attacks are something that happens to you like a contraction.

Client: Yea! I quite like that analogy!

Counselor: Yes. I like it too. So, how are you feeling so far about today's session?

Client: Yea good. It's helped. I feel like I am slowly getting myself back together ready to try again. I knew I would. I knew I just needed a bit of time and needed to get my head straight and then I would be able to try again. I think I'm quite good like that. After a few days I always get my fight back.

Counselor: So it helps to just take a few days rest, think things through and then you, once again, feel ready to work on feeling calmer when outside.

Client: Yes.

Counselor: Is there anything else you think we need to discuss during this session?

Client: No, not really. I feel I have my tool kit ready to go. To try and do the next steps.

Counselor: What will your next steps be?

(I want to clarify the next steps so the client has these clearly in mind. I find the more specific the goal, the more likely it is that the client will attempt it.)

Client: I think walking to the bottom of the road and back would be good.

Counselor: How confident do you feel about that now, on a scale of 0 to 10, 0 being not very confident at all and 10 being very confident?

Client: About a 6. Ah! That's my magic number.

Counselor: So during this session you have gone from a 5 to a 6.

Client: Yes, I have. That feels good. After that walk I feel a bit more confident now. I think I can definitely get to the bottom of the road and back next time.

Counselor: Great. How will you decide what your next steps are after the walk to the bottom of the road and back?

Client: I think I will just know what I feel capable of trying next. I would like to get to the shop and back.

Counselor: Ah yes. You've said that before. We are nearing the end of our session here today. Would you like to have another session?

Client: Yes. Yes please.

Counselor: When would you like the next session? Some clients find it helpful to have the first few sessions fairly close together as you have done, one a week, and then the subsequent sessions are a bit more spaced out to allow you time to practice the strategies we have discussed.

Client: That sounds a good idea. I feel like I know what I need to do now. I have a plan and I guess now it's just implementing that plan.

Counselor: When do you think you would like your next session?

Client: Maybe in two weeks or a month? What do most people do?

Counselor: Everyone is different. Some people continue to have weekly, others do the third session in a fortnight and then move on to monthly after that.

Client: Yes that's good. I would like to go for that please. That way if I have a setback or fail I haven't got too long to wait to talk it all through.

Counselor: That's fine. So two weeks today, same time, same place?

Client: Yes.

Counselor: What would need to be happening for you to come to my offices for your session?

(I want to know when the client will feel ready to come to my offices. Talking about it gets the client thinking about it and at least considering it as a possible future activity. There is no pressure on the client.)

Client: I need to feel quite a lot better. If I can't make it to the shop, then I can't make it your offices. Sorry.

Counselor: No, it's absolutely fine. I'm just wondering what will be happening in your life, where would you be in relation to your original goal, that would make you feel confident enough to visit me at my offices?

Client: Hmm... I suppose if I was going to the shop on my own, maybe even if I was driving a little bit again. I might feel more confident if I was driving again as that way I can drive to your offices rather than walk. That would feel more comfortable to me.

Counselor: What would make you feel confident enough to drive again?

Client: I don't know.

Counselor: Is there anything that we have learned so far that we could apply to you feeling confident enough to drive again?

Client: The small steps!

Counselor: How would you feel about driving to the end of your road and back?

Client: Easy. Real easy. I'd do it in about 10 seconds.

Counselor: How would you feel about driving around the block?

Client: Not so easy! I don't think I could do that.

Counselor: What do you think is the most that you could do?

Client: Down to the end of my road and then down to the next road and then turn back and come home.

Counselor: On the 0 to 10 scale, 0 being not very confident at all and 10 being very confident, how confident are you that you could drive to the end of your road and then the next road and then return home?

Client: About a 7.

Counselor: Is that confident enough to try it?

Client: Yes! Wow. I can't believe that I am even thinking about driving my car again! I thought it would be months before I even considered it but the small steps thing makes me feel like I don't have to wait! I would love to get back driving my car again. I feel so trapped in the house. If I could drive my car again, then I could go and visit my mum and my friends and my sister. It would be so nice getting out of the house again and getting some of my independence back. It would feel just so nice.

Counselor: What difference would that make to you?

Client: I'd feel like I was getting my life back. Like I was getting towards somewhere near normal.

Counselor: And what difference would that make?

Client: I'd just feel so happy. Like a weight had been lifted off me.

Counselor: So taking the small step of driving down to the end of your road and then the next road and coming back home would be the first step towards achieving this?

Client: Yes. Definitely.

Counselor: Great. Well, as before I would just like to take a few moments to read through my notes from the session so I can feedback to you and we can agree on the next steps. Is that okay with you?

Client: Yes. Yes of course.

Counselor looks through notes.

Counselor: Sorry, that took me a bit longer than usual. We have covered quite a bit in today's session.

Client: Yes, it's been good.

Counselor: Firstly, once again I am really impressed with your determination. Even though you had a difficult week you were still willing to work with me today. I liked the fact that you recognized that after a failure or setback you know that you need to take a few days out, think things through and then you will be ready to fight it again.

I was also really impressed that after last week's session, when you were feeling calm and confident, that you used the opportunity to carry out your next step of walking to the end of the road and back, plus your 10 steps.

I think it was great that in today's session you walked half way down the road, felt okay, and continued a little further. Once again you were being spontaneous and using the opportunity of feeling okay to progress to the next step.

In this session you have recognized patterns and have been able to apply what you have learned elsewhere to new activities. Like the driving idea. You broke down the task of driving into small steps and knew what your first step would be.

You came up with a 'failure plan' of if you fail or experience a setback, you will do a small step that feels easy to you. You mentioned that you felt you would progress through the steps a lot quicker the second time round as you had already done the steps once before.

You discovered that your first panic attack is the worst and then they get less severe. You likened them to contractions. Something you had to put up with for a few minutes before it passed. Once again you recognized that distractions help. We talked about different things you could think about and you came up with the idea of thinking about decorating the rooms in your house and garden, playing the chords on your guitar or calling someone.

Client: Oh yes. I forgot about that.

Counselor: We have decided that we will meet in two weeks time to give you time to try out the strategies we have discussed today.

Client: Yes. Hearing it all back makes me realize how much we have covered. You feel like you are just chatting but actually you are creating a plan of sorts.

Counselor: Yes. How does that all feel to you?

Client: Yea good. I just hope I can put it into practice!

Counselor: How do you feel about making a note of the positive changes you experience during the next fortnight? Noting down what positive change happened and what you were feeling and thinking.

(It can really help the client to note down what activities they have tried and what they were thinking and feeling at the time. This helps to identify thinking patterns and possible solutions. At the end, the book becomes a book of solutions.)

Client: Oops. I was supposed to do that before wasn't I? I did start the next day but after my horrible day I totally forgot. To be honest there wasn't much to report after Thursday anyway.

Counselor: As it's a fortnight you might find it helpful to keep a bit of a log. With that length of time it can be difficult to recall some of the positive changes in the earlier week.

Client: Yes. Should I put my failures in there too?

Counselor: If you think that would be helpful. If you are going to write about your failures note down what you were thinking or feeling before the setback. I'd like you to note how you cope with those failures. How do you get your confidence back again? Also note if there was anything you did during the setback that prevented it from getting worse.

Client: I'm not sure I can remember all of that!

Counselor: What would help you to remember?

Client: Writing it down. I'll note it down in my phone while I remember.

Counselor: So note positive changes and what you were thinking or feeling at the time. If you note failures, note what you were thinking or feeling. Note how you coped and how you got your confidence back again. Also note if there was anything you did during the setback that prevented it from getting worse.

(This last sentence is to help the client recognize what they did do that helped in that situation. Once again there may be possible solutions here or at the very least techniques to prevent setbacks.)

Client: Right, that's all in there.

Counselor: That's it for today then.

Client: Great, thanks very much.

Counselor: You're welcome.

Counseling session ends.

Session Four

Counselor: Hi

Client: Hi

Counselor: How are you?

Client: Good. Come in.

Counselor: Thanks.

Both sit down in the lounge.

Counselor: So, how has your fortnight been?

Client: It's been good, really good.

Counselor: Excellent. What's happened?

Client: You are not going to believe this but I drove to my Mums!

Counselor: That is great news!

Client: You should have seen her face when she answered the door. It took her a few minutes to get her head around it. She couldn't believe I was standing there.

Counselor: What did she say?

Client: She was just so pleased! I went in and had a cup of tea with her and piece of cake. After about half an hour I left. I started to feel anxious and wanted to make sure that I could get home okay. I didn't want to have a panic attack while I was driving. But I was so pleased with myself!

Counselor: That's great. How far away does your mum live?

Client: It's about a 6 minute drive if there is no traffic.

Counselor: It's really great. How did you decide to drive to your mums?

Client: I decided to drive to the end of the road and the next road like we said. I went at 11am in the morning as I figured there wouldn't be much traffic at that time. I had in the back of my mind that if I felt well then I might drive to mums. I didn't really want to admit it to myself that this was my ultimate goal as I didn't want to fail. But having it just there lingering in the back of mind as a possible meant that when I got to my goal post of the end of the next road, I had somewhere else to go if I felt like I could.

Counselor: I'm really impressed that you had the foresight to consider what the following step would be but without putting pressure on yourself. How did you do that?

Client: I think just not saying it out loud. I don't know that I want to have a bigger goal in mind all the time because if I finished my first goal and then didn't feel up to the bigger goal, I'd feel like I had failed whereas actually I had done well and achieved the first goal.

Counselor: So how can we make sure that doesn't happen?

Client: I'm not sure. It's tricky to know how to do that.

Counselor: Do you have any ideas? We could just think of some ideas and evaluate them afterwards.

Client: Maybe I pre-plan all the bigger goals now. That way I will know what my next steps are.

Counselor: How would that make you feel, having all of your goals listed ready?

Client: I don't think I'd like it. I think I'd realize or feel that I have a long way to go to get better.

Counselor: Okay, what other options do we have?

Client: I don't know.

Silence.

Client: I can't really think of anything else. I guess I could just do what I did last week and have a rough idea what I might do if I feel good after achieving the initial goal. I think not telling anyone about my goals helped.

Counselor: So you didn't tell anyone you were planning to drive your car or that you might go and see your mum?

Client: That's right. That way if I don't feel up to it and decide not to do it, I don't have to feel as bad about it. I only have myself to answer to rather than having to justify or defend myself to others.

Counselor: Okay.

Client: It also helps because that way I am not admitting the bigger goals to myself either.

Counselor: Okay.

Client: I know. It sounds weird doesn't it?

Counselor: As long as it works for you that's all we want.

Client: True. I think it is really important that I don't focus on the big goal. I want to still feel the achievement of the smaller goal if I manage to achieve it. But then saying that out loud of course I am still going to feel a sense of achievement. If I walk an extra 10 steps but don't make the 20 steps I had as my bigger goal, it's still 10 more steps than I did previously. I must remember to focus on what I did do rather than what I didn't.

Counselor: So it's going to be important that you focus on your initial goal first and foremost and to celebrate the success you have with that. The bigger goal is just another possible...

Client: Yea, like a bonus. That's quite a nice way of looking at it. I can look at it as the bigger goal is a bonus goal.

Counselor: Great. I think it's really good that you are foreseeing what you might feel in this situation.

Client: Thanks.

Counselor: So you drove to your mums this week which is a big achievement. I know that you said having the smaller goal in mind first helped you achieve this. What else helped?

Client: I think these last few weeks knowing that my panic attacks get less has really helped. I was a bit worried about having a panic attack while driving because that might not be very safe.

(I'm concerned that the client might have a panic attack whilst driving and this might not be very safe for other road users. The client is clearly concerned about this too. I think this needs to be addressed in this session.)

Counselor: Have you ever had a panic attack while driving?

Client: Yes! Quite a few! That is why I don't drive anymore. Well until last week anyway. It's so frightening. I can't be safe on the roads if I'm panicking.

Counselor: So when you previously had panic attacks whilst driving, what happened?

Client: What do you mean? I was just sat at the traffic lights and then the panic attack would come.

Counselor: Right. And how did you cope?

Client: Well I didn't. I didn't cope very well at all. That's why I hate driving.

Counselor: So what happened? Talk me through it. You were sat at the traffic lights and you started having a panic attack.

Client: Yea. I thought 'oh my, oh my I can't cope. I can't cope with this.' And I probably felt all hot and sticky and like I am going to pass out.

Counselor: And then what happened?

Client: Well. It passed and the traffic lights changed and I carried on driving.

Counselor: So you had a panic attack in your car whilst stationary at lights. It passed and you carried on driving.

Client: Yes. I went home.

Counselor: Can you talk me through the other panic attacks you have experienced whilst driving. Did they always happen at traffic lights or did they sometimes happen when you were actually driving?

(I am trying to break driving down into different chunks. I want to know if the panic attacks happened at certain times.)

Client: Hmm... Let me think. I think they always happened at traffic lights actually.

Counselor: So if you have a panic attack whilst driving it is unlikely to happen when you are actually moving?

Client: Yea. You could put it like that. I'm okay when I'm moving. I guess it's because I don't feel trapped. At traffic lights I feel trapped. I can't go anywhere.

Counselor: So your fear of driving is that you will have a panic attack and not be safe on the roads. You don't want to panic whilst driving. You only seem to have panic attacks whilst stationary at traffic lights. Let's imagine that you are at the traffic lights and you are having a panic attack and the lights change. What happens next?

Client: I drive off.

Counselor: What happens to the panic attack?

Client: It stops. I'm moving again and feel okay again.

Counselor: So you only experience panic attacks whilst stationary?

Client: Yes. Ah! And if I have a panic attack whilst stationary, I can't harm anyone driving can I? I think when I used to drive and was having a panic attack at the lights, once the lights changed I was okay. It felt a little strange driving in those first few seconds but then after that I felt fine.

Counselor: So we know that you only panic whilst stationary. As you are stationary, you can't harm anyone. You are safe.

Client: Yes.

Counselor: Do you have panic attacks every time you are at traffic lights?

Client: No.

Counselor: How often?

Client: I suppose...I...it's hard to quantify. I guess that I've only ever had 3 or 4 panic attacks whilst driving. But that was enough!

Counselor: So you have occasionally had a panic attack whist driving?

(I want the client to clarify how often she has panic attacks at traffic lights. I don't want her to over generalize that she always has panic attacks at traffic lights as this type of thinking could bring on the panic attacks. I want her to find what the actual truth is. I have summarized the fact that she has only had 3 or 4 panic attacks at the traffic lights with the word occasionally. Hopefully with this thought in mind she will realize that she only panics occasionally and this truth will help her to feel calmer.)

Client: Yes. This is making me feel a bit better about things. If I have a panic attack, it's likely to be at the traffic lights whilst stationary. As soon as I'm moving it will disappear again. And I only have them occasionally. Actually a better word would be rarely. I only have them rarely at traffic lights. It's not like I have them every time I stop at traffic lights.

Counselor: How do you feel about driving now?

Client: A bit more confident. A bit anxious still. Well, actually still fairly anxious. I guess I just need to do more practice. Keep practicing the driving.

Counselor: I really like that you are using the word practicing. I think that's a nice way to look at it.

Client: If I say I am practicing, then I am less likely to be upset that I failed as it was only a practice!

Counselor: I like it! So we have addressed your driving. Is there anything else we should be talking about today?

Client: Hmm... Let me think.

Silence.

Client: I can't really think of anything. I think I have all the strategies in place now. I know what I am doing. I just need to go out there and do it.

Counselor: How did you get on with your notes on the positive changes you were experiencing in the last few weeks?

Client: Ah yes, I did that. I'll go and get it.

Client goes off to find her notebook.

Client: Shall I just pass this to you to read?

Counselor: No that's okay. It's your book. Maybe you could just use it to jog your memory of what you tried and what helped or did not help.

Client: Okay. I'll look through. Oh yes. In the first week I also went for another walk around the block with Rob. I didn't think I would be able to do that again for ages as last time we got into that argument when he wouldn't take me home.

Counselor: I remember. What notes did you make?

Client: I'll read them. Felt good this evening. Felt strong and decided to go for a walk with Rob. Planned to just go to the end of the road and back but we ended up going for a long walk down to the railway station. Grabbed some chocolate at the shops!

Counselor: So you were feeling strong. What was helping you to feel strong?

(If she knows what makes her feel strong, maybe she can repeat this and she can feel strong more often.)

Client: Nothing in particular. I guess that I just felt strong and so used it and went out. It felt really nice being in the shop and choosing a chocolate bar. It's a small thing I know but to me it's quite a big deal. I was picturing at the back of mind that if I made it to the shop I'd buy myself a bag of minstrels. I think that actually spurred me on.

Counselor: So having some kind of reward at the end helped to spur you on?

Client: Yes, yes I think it did.

Counselor: Could you use that in other situations?

Client: I can't keep eating chocolate as I'll put weight on.

Counselor: So maybe not chocolate but some other treat? It doesn't have to food related!

Client: Like what?

Counselor: I was going to ask you that question! Let's think about what treats you could reward yourself with. Some people reward themselves with watching their favorite movie or eating their favorite dinner.

Client: I'm not sure that would work for me.

Counselor: That's good. It's good that you recognize what will and won't work for you.

Client: For me it would have to be chocolate or a sugary treat!

Counselor: What shall we say about treats then?

Client: Maybe if I do 3 or 4 things then I get a treat. A piece of cake or something.

Counselor: Okay, if you like that idea you could do that.

Client: I might do. I'm not sure.

Counselor: So back to your notes. What else have you got written down?

Client: I'll have a look. Oh yea, I forgot about this too. I was feeling confident and tried to walk to the shop on my own. As I was about to leave I started to feel anxious and short of breath, like I couldn't breathe. I did some deep breathing but it didn't help. It never does.

(Talking through the times when the client felt anxious or tried something that didn't help can also be a learning point.)

Counselor: Talk me through your deep breathing. What do you do?

Client: I breathe in for four, 1...2...3...4 and out for four, 1...2...3...4 and see I feel it now. I feel light-headed.

Counselor: So breathing in and out for 4 doesn't help.

Client: No. I don't know why I even tried it.

Counselor: You said that as you were about to leave you started to feel anxious. Did you note down what you were thinking about at the time?

Client: No. But I think I was thinking I can't do this. What if I get down there and I can't get back.

Counselor: Let's think this through. What would you have done if that was the case?

(I want the client to think through their fears. If she can have a plan in place this could help her to feel calmer.)

Client: I don't know. I would have called mum to see if she could pick me up but what if she wasn't there and I was stuck there. I would be trapped.

Counselor: So let's imagine this worst case scenario and you have made it to the shop but you can't get back. What would you have done? What could you remind yourself of that would help in this situation?

Client: I would just start walking towards home. I would just set myself a target of 10 steps. I would tell myself that the first panic attack is the worst and then they will get less.

Counselor: Is there anything else that you could have done in this situation that would have helped you to feel calmer about leaving the house?

Client: What about if I had spoken to my mum to check she was in? Then I could tell her that I am going to walk to the shop and if I needed to, I could call her to come and get me. That would make me feel a lot calmer. It would be like a back-up plan.

Counselor: So last week when you were planning to go to the shop, on a scale of 0 to 10, 0 being not very confident and 10 being very confident, how confident were you?

Client: About a 2.

Counselor: Now let's imagine that you have called your mum and she is ready to pick you up if you need her to. You are about to leave for the shops. How confident do you feel now? 0 being not very confident and 10 being confident.

Client: 7, yeah a 6 or probably a 7. I feel I could do it. But I don't want to have to rely on others all the time. I'd like to be able to do it myself.

Counselor: So you'd like to be able to do it yourself without your Mum being involved. However, in order to help build your confidence would it be okay to have your Mum ready to pick you up at least to begin with?

Client: Yes, maybe if I had Mum on stand-by for the first few times and then the next time I do it myself.

Counselor: How confident will you need to be before you can walk to the shop and back on your own without your mum on stand-by? 0 to 10 scale, 0 not very confident and 10 very confident.

Client: 6 or probably a 7 as it feels quite a big deal to me.

Counselor: So you feel confident enough now to try walking to the shop on your own with your mum on stand-by. Then once you feel confident enough, maybe a 6 or a 7, you will then attempt it on your own.

Client: Yes, I like that idea. I like that I'll practice it with my mum on stand-by. That takes quite a lot of the pressure off.

Counselor: Do you think this solution could be applied elsewhere?

Client: Yes. For example if I was to drive to my friends, I could have mum on stand-by. If I felt bad whilst driving, I could pull over somewhere safe and get her to come and get me. Just park my car somewhere and Rob could pick it up later for me.

Counselor: Is your friend's house far away?

Client: It's about a 20 minute drive. My reward would be seeing my friend! I'd take over some cookies or something.

Counselor: How would it make you feel to drive to your friend's house and spend some time with her?

Client: Amazing. I'd feel just great.

Counselor: So it seems that you have come up with another strategy to help push yourself further than you would if you were just going out on your own with no back-up.

Client: Yea, it's a way to push myself that bit further but still feeling relatively calm about things. Well as calm as I can feel.

Counselor: Are you finding going through your notes helpful? Shall we continue?

Client: Yes, it helps thinking it all through.

Counselor: What's next?

Client: There's not too much more in here really. I've pretty much spoken about everything I tried. I did go to my Dads though. He came and picked me up and we just went to his for a couple of hours. It was nice to get out of the house for a bit.

Counselor: How calm were you at your Dads on a scale of 0 to 10, 0 being not very calm and 10 being very calm?

Client: Oh that was easy, about a 9.5 or a 10. It didn't bother me at all.

Counselor: What was it about that situation that made you feel so calm?

Client: I just felt safe. I wasn't out in the street. I was just in his car. Nobody could see me. Then I was at his house and felt fine.

Counselor: Do you think you could have done this 4 weeks ago?

Client: Um... no probably not. It just seemed easy compared to what I have been doing.

(I picked up that the client mentioned that it was because nobody could see her. I wonder if this thought is holding her back and I want to address it with her.)

Counselor: You mentioned that it was easy because nobody could see you. What concerns you about people seeing you? What difference does it make to you?

Client: If I'm out, people will see me be sick or faint.

Counselor: Has that ever happened when you had a panic attack?

Client: Well, no. But that's what I think is going to happen.

Counselor: But you are never sick and you never faint whilst having a panic attack. You are always okay?

Client: Yes, I'm always okay. That's something else I can say to myself isn't it? I'm always okay. I think, I think that I am actually ill though. That it's not a panic attack and that I am actually ill and therefore I am going to be sick or pass out. When I was at school I fainted. I felt really sick in class and then asked a friend to come with me to the sick bay. I then fainted outside the door. It made me realize that I wasn't invincible. I always used to think 'I'll be okay' and go out even if I felt really poorly. But that made me lose my confidence. It made me think that I need to be careful when I go out. That I need to be aware that I might actually be ill. I think that's where all this comes from you know.

(Sometimes the client can reveal an event that they found disturbing in their past that contributes to their present day fears. It may take a few sessions before the client mentions it.)

Counselor: Okay. It sounds like you had an experience that you fear will happen again?

Client: Yes. It's just made me feel frightened. You know? I don't want that to happen again.

(I want the client to think through her beliefs on the situation. I also want her to adopt some healthy thinking patterns about her fear of it happening again.)

Counselor: What are your beliefs on this? When you go out, how strongly do you believe that you are actually ill? If 0 was you are not ill and 10 was you are actually ill, where are you on the scale?

Client: About a 2. I know I'm not really ill. Sometimes I feel slightly differently with my anxiety and I think 'oh I am actually ill this time because this feels different' but I read somewhere that you shouldn't be frightened of every new sensation. Anxiety can often feel a little different to the time before.

Counselor: Do you say that to yourself sometimes?

Client: Yes I try to but sometimes I forget.

Counselor: What could help you to remember?

Client: I feel almost like I need a little prompt sheet to read to cover everything that we have talked about. I could note down all my strategies and then read them before I leave the house. That way they are fresh in my mind.

Counselor: I think that's a really good idea. When will you do that?

Client: I could do it today after you leave. Write down everything that we have spoken about that I can remember.

Counselor: Do you think you can remember the strategies?

Client: Yes I think so. Maybe you can check them the next time I see you. Off the top of my head they are small steps that feel easy, go out spontaneously, carry on further whilst out if I still feel good, have a bigger goal in the back of mind but don't focus on it too much, have Mum on stand-by to help me achieve bigger goals, if I fail go back to a smaller goal that feels really easy for me to do to get my confidence back, when driving realize that I am fine whilst in motion so am not a danger to other road users as I only rarely panic at traffic lights, what else?

Counselor: Panic attacks?

Client: Yes, panic attacks only last a few minutes and they get less and less, they are like contractions I just have to wait for them to pass. The strategies I have got don't sound much when I say them all out loud but they are working for me.

Counselor: That's what these sessions are all about. Different people need different solutions. It's about finding out what works for you. Looking at what helps and what doesn't help.

Client: The biggest thing for me is the small steps and increasing it gradually. Keep everything feeling really easy. If I have to keep repeating a step, then I have to keep repeating it. Having this in mind takes the pressure off me and I keep ending up doing more than I anticipated!

Counselor: Yes, I think for you the small steps idea has really helped you to start getting out and about again.

Client: Definitely. Just keep it as easy small steps. I can build on this over time. As long as I am going in the right direction. I do get frustrated sometimes thinking that this is going to take me ages but then I wonder if once I start getting better, it will naturally speed up. I'll feel more and more comfortable to do bigger and bigger steps.

Counselor: Yes, you could definitely find that. Is there anything else you would like to talk about? We have a little while left for this session.

Client: Yes, I keep thinking through what if I actually am ill? How would I cope? What would I actually do if I went out and it wasn't the anxiety and I was actually sick or fainted? How would I cope with that? It frightens me and I think that if I could have a plan in place to deal with it, that might help me quite a bit.

Counselor: Okay, we can have a think about that.

Client: Great.

Counselor: Do you have any strategies in mind? Have you thought about a plan already?

(I want to check what the client has already thought of. People naturally try to solve their problems and I suspect that she has already thought of some possible solutions.)

Client: Well, I figure that if I do get ill when I am out, I would just call someone to come and get me.

Counselor: Okay.

Client: But what if I was away from home on my own? Say I got better and I was in London. What would I do then? Nobody could come and get me. Well they could but it would take them a couple of hours. What would I do?

Counselor: Can you think of any options?

Client: Not really.

Counselor: What do you think other people might do if they are away from home and are unwell?

(It can help to think what other people would think or do in a situation. This helps to get some rational beliefs in mind that the client can then adopt as their own. It can be easier for the client to think of solutions for other people than solutions for herself.)

Client: They could get a hotel room?

Counselor: Yes, I'm sure some of them would get a hotel room and go and lie down for a bit.

Client: So I could book a hotel room and rest up until I felt better.

Counselor: Yes.

Client: What if I was on the journey? Like on a train or something?

Counselor: Any ideas? What might other people do or think in that situation?

Client: That they just have to get through that journey and get home. It's probably only a few hours max. Or they could get off the train if they felt really bad and catch a cab the rest of the way home. Or call ahead and get someone to meet them in a couple of stations time to take them home.

Counselor: Yes any of those could work.

Client: So if it did happen, which is unlikely, I could cope. Just like anyone else. I might feel terrible for a few hours but it's only a few hours and then I'd be home.

Counselor: Yes. Does that help? Does it help to know what you would do in that situation?

Client: Yes. I keep feeling like I need to have a plan. Like if I have a plan, then I don't have to think too much in that situation because I already know what to do. I know it sounds silly thinking all of this through. Most people wouldn't need to. They would just be okay and they would just cope.

Counselor: Everyone is different. Do you like to plan generally? Do you prefer knowing what you are going to do?

Client: Yes, I prefer to know what I'm doing. I am a bit of a planner. I'd like to be more flexible but I'm just not. I've always been a planner.

Counselor: I think if planning works for you, then that's all that matters.

Client: Do you think?

Counselor: Yes I do. So how does that feel now that you have a plan?

Client: Better. If I'm local and I am actually ill then I just call someone I know to come and get me. I could cope for the few minutes whilst I wait for them. If I am away from home, once I'm a bit better, I can stay in a hotel, grab a cab home or just put up with the journey home. It would depend on when I felt unwell. Ultimately I would cope. I'd be okay.

Counselor: Great. We are nearing the end of the session now. Has this session been helpful to you?

Client: Yes, the only bit I wasn't sure on was the rewards bit. I know it might work for some but I'm not sure it could work for me. Not all the time anyway. Maybe if I use rewards now again? Yes, maybe that could work.

Counselor: So the rewards section didn't quite feel right to you. It's good that you can recognize this. But you may use a reward now and again, as you see fit.

Client: Yes.

Counselor: Right, well I would like to look through my notes and summarize the session back to you and agree on the next steps. Is that okay with you?

Client: Yes of course.

Counselor looks through notes.

Counselor: I think we have covered quite a lot in this session. I really appreciated your honesty during the session. I was impressed that you could recognize what may or may not work for you and how you anticipated what you might think in different situations.

You are still finding it helpful to break things down into small steps that feel easy for you. You are finding that this can apply to lots of different situations, one being driving. You suggested that you might be able to achieve larger goals if you had your Mum as back-up. We discussed it was helpful to focus on small initial goals and to have a larger goal in the back of your mind, being careful to focus primarily on the initial goal and to celebrate your successes of the initial goal.

We spoke about driving and discovered that whilst actually moving you never have a panic attack and therefore you are safe to drive. We spoke about a plan of what to do if you actually were taken ill and you know that you would cope and would either call someone to collect you, stay in a hotel if you were away from home or you would just put up with feeling unwell until you made it home.

We spoke about the possibility of you driving to see your friend with your Mum on stand-by and how great this would feel for you.

Client: Yes. It feels like the lessons I am learning are really getting consolidated now. Small steps, small steps, small steps! And a stand-by back-up plan of my Mum!

Counselor: I think you are making really good progress. Would you like to have another meeting?

Client: Yes please. Maybe I could do it in a month's time, give me time to practice what I have been learning. I think if I do a month's worth of work, then I will have lots to talk to you about.

Counselor: Sounds like a good idea to me. So shall we say four weeks time, same time?

Client: Yes.

Counselor: Shall we say that I am coming to you?

Client: Yes, for now. Maybe if I feel well enough I could call you to arrange to come to your offices instead? Now I'm saying that I don't think I will be able to. It seems too bigger step.

Counselor: That's fine. Let's say that I will come to you but if you want to change it and feel like you want to come to my office that's fine. Just give me a call.

Client: Great, thanks.

Counselor: In between now and the next session I would like you to continue to notice the positive changes. You can continue to write them in your notebook if you like.

Client: I'll do that, especially as I won't see you for a month. That's a long time and I might forget quite a bit of it.

Counselor: Great. Right, I shall be off then.

Client: Thanks very much.

Counselor: You're welcome.

Counseling session ends.

Session Five

Counselor: Hello.

Client: Hello.

Counselor: Please, come in.

Client: Thanks.

Counselor: We're just in the room at the top of the stairs.

Client: Thanks.

Both client and counselor take a seat in the counseling room.

Counselor: So, I was really pleased to get your call yesterday saying that you wanted to come to my offices.

Client: Yea, I just felt able to do it. I've done so much this month that this felt like just one more thing that I could do. It's all good practice.

Counselor: So you've had a good month?

Client: Yea, it's been great. It's not to say there haven't been ups and downs. I have had my fair share of tears this month. Tears of frustration but after each setback, I have been quick to get back to going out again.

Counselor: What's helped you to do that?

Client: I've just tried to remind myself that I'm getting better. I look at how far I've come and try to appreciate how well I am doing. You know even coming here. I would not have even dreamed of being able to do this two months ago and today doesn't feel like that bigger deal. It's not like I have had to psyche myself up for today or I have seen it as a massive challenge. It just felt within my grasp, within my capabilities.

Counselor: That's really good to hear. So reminding yourself how far you have come has helped you to overcome your feelings of frustration?

Client: Yes, it's helped me to overcome my feelings of frustration when I am just thinking negatively. Like I think I will never get better and it's pointless even trying to get better. Or it's going to take me months and months to get better and I just want to be better now. Immediately.

Counselor: So you are able to talk yourself out of your negative mindset?

Client: Yes. Before it was usually about two days before I felt able to try and go outside again but just lately it hasn't been so long. I'd say most of the time I'm able to feel okay to go out again the next day or sometimes even later the same day. Other times, I think it's only happened once or maybe twice, I need a few days to lick my wounds.

Counselor: Was there anything in particular that you did or did not do that led you to feel you needed a few days to recover?

Client: I'm not sure. It seemed random but there were a few occasions when I went out and I just felt anxious the whole time. Really on edge. I didn't actually have a panic attack but it was a real struggle just being out. It was like I was really having to fight it. I was having to fight my way through it. I was annoyed at myself for feeling that anxious and it took me a few days to want to go out again.

Counselor: During those occasions when you felt anxious, how did you cope?

Client: I had spoken to my mum about the anxiety. We had got into quite a deep conversation about it. She said that you can't let it win. When I told her about feeling anxious and how I was disappointed in myself for feeling it, she said it is takes more courage to feel anxious and remain in the situation than if you didn't feel anxious at all. And I think that rings true for me. It's just annoying. She also reminded me of how far I have come which helped. She made me feel like it wasn't so bad. That I was doing okay.

Counselor: How did that make you feel?

Client: Like I was doing okay. That sometimes I might feel anxious and there might not be any reason for it and I just need to have the courage to stay in the situation and not run away. I haven't this month. I haven't run away from any situations. I have put up with my anxiety and just gritted my teeth and tried to carry on as normal. It wasn't easy but I did it.

Counselor: Even though you felt anxious you managed to carry on with whatever you were doing?

Client: Yes.

Counselor: What helped you to do that?

Client: My mum's words ringing in my ears.

Counselor: Anything else?

Client: Knowing that it was just anxiety. That it could only last so long. That's something else my mum said to me. She said that your body can't remain in that anxious state for very long as you become exhausted. It can only last so long. That helped too.

Counselor: What else?

Client: Knowing that if I did have panic attacks they would only last a few minutes and they'd get less. I'd be okay.

Counselor: Great. So thinking about today's session what are your best hopes for today's session? What would you like to get out of it?

Client: I'm not sure really. I mean, I guess I could talk you through my notes and everything I've done, what I was thinking and feeling at the time.

Counselor: Would you like to do that?

Client: I've kind of done it myself really. I read through all of my notes and I can see what helps me and what doesn't. I found myself picturing negative events again while I was out and then remembered that I should be picturing myself a few minutes up the road and feeling fine.

Counselor: What difference did that make, thinking about yourself succeeding?

Client: A big difference. I just need to keep remembering it. When I look back at my notes though I can see where I'm going wrong.

Counselor: And right?

Client: Yes and where I'm going right!

Counselor: So it seems that that side of things are okay for you.

Client: Yes, I don't really know what else we can talk about. I kind of feel like we have done all the talking and now it's more about the action. I'd like to tell you everything I've done if that's okay?

Counselor: Of course. I would like to hear it!

Client: I'll just look at my notes and read some of the things I did then. I drove to my friends and stayed for tea and cookies!

Counselor: Great!

Client: I then went to another friends too. I've been out with Rob to his family's house for dinner, I haven't done that in ages. I managed to eat my dinner too which I thought I might struggle with but was fine. I walked to the shop and back on my own a few times with Mum as back-up! Me and Rob went for a drive down to the coast one evening and had a short walk along the seafront. It was beautiful. I even went into a department store in the city. We drove and parked in their car park and had a quick look round. Well actually we were probably in there about 30 minutes. We went when it was quiet on a Thursday evening. It feels so good to just be in these places again. There's lots more I did but they were the highlights!

Counselor: Excellent. So I'm wondering what would be helpful today?

Client: I don't know. I feel like I have a handle on everything and I just need to keep building up what I am doing.

Counselor: So what else would you like to achieve? What are your next steps?

Client: I've not really thought about them. Although I have been thinking that I might like to volunteer locally. Something to do with children or animals. Perhaps working in the charity shop. I am starting to feel like I might be able to do it. I wondered if I spoke to them about my anxiety and ask to just do one hour here and there and then perhaps build it up. Oh, I don't know if I could do it yet.

Counselor: When do you think you will be able to do it? What else would be happening?

Client: I'm not sure. I think I would need to have achieved maybe a few more goals first.

Counselor: What specific goals would you need to achieve before you felt ready to consider volunteering?

Client: Maybe if I could go to town for an hour or so.

Counselor: What would help you to achieve that?

Client: How would I achieve going into town?

Counselor: Yes.

Client: Don't know. I don't feel ready yet.

Counselor: On the scale of 0 to 10, 0 being not ready at all and 10 being ready, where are you on the scale today?

Client: Probably about a 4.

Counselor: Where would you need to be to try going into town?

Client: Probably a 7.

Counselor: So you are a 4 now. What would be happening at a 5?

Client: I think I would have just practiced what I am doing a bit more. Ah! I've had an idea. Why don't I build it up again? Take a small step and build on that. So last time I went to one shop. How about next time I go to two shops? Build it up like that. That way it will feel easy to me.

Counselor: Good idea. So how ready do you feel to go to two shops in town, 0 being not ready at all and 10 being ready?

Client: Oh I think that would be fairly easy. I'd say probably an 8. I've already done one shop so to do one more shop would be pretty easy. I say that but I will still probably feel anxious but I know I can do it. Well I think I can do it.

Counselor: Do you feel anxious all the time when you are out?

Client: Usually.

(The client used the word 'usually'. This tells me that there might be exceptions. There may be times with the client is out when she doesn't feel anxious. She already mentioned that she felt calm going to her Dads. I want to know more about the times that she feels calm and what she is doing or thinking about at this time.)

Counselor: So there are some times when you don't feel anxious when you are out?

Client: Yes, like when I am doing the easy stuff. Like walking round the block with Rob. I've done it probably about 5 times now. I know I can do it and am pretty confident about it. Sometimes I feel a little anxious just before we leave but actually feel fine when I am out.

Counselor: And how do you feel about planning activities now? You have mentioned that you find it easier when you can be spontaneous. How do you feel about planning an activity now?

Client: Hmm... I'm not sure. I am still doing everything spontaneously. Literally with my friends I just phoned them up and said are you free? Can I come over?

Counselor: So on the scale of 0 to 10, 0 being not ready and 10 being ready, how ready do you feel to plan an activity?

Client: Only about a 4.

Counselor: What would you need to feel? Where on the scale would you need to be 0 being not ready and 10 being ready?

Client: I'd need to be a 6.

Counselor: How could we get you to a 6?

Client: I don't know. I just think that if I know what I am going to do, I will panic.

Counselor: What can we use from what has worked elsewhere?

Client: Oh, maybe a small step. Maybe I plan something really, really small. Maybe I say to Rob in the morning about going out for a walk that evening and see how I get on. Then if I can do that, perhaps plan something else small which is maybe two days in advance. Or I could do it the other way and plan a bigger step later on the in the day.

Counselor: What do you think will help you to manage the time in between making the arrangement and you actually doing the activity?

Client: I guess I'll need to keep my thoughts positive.

Counselor: What will you say to yourself?

Client: That I can do it. That I'll be okay.

Counselor: What else could help?

Client: Keeping myself distracted. If I only attempt a simple goal, something really, really easy at first then I don't think I would worry about doing it.

Counselor: Can you give me an example?

Client: Like planning that I will walk 10 steps outside of my front drive tomorrow morning. That's easy.

Counselor: How confident are you that you could do that, 0 being not very confident and 10 being very confident?

Client: A 10!

(I want the client to commit to the goal so I ask her if she is planning to commit to the goal.)

Counselor: Will you plan to do that then?

Client: Yes. That can be the first step to planning to go out and then I can just build up like I have built up going out spontaneously.

Counselor: Good. Sounds like a plan.

Client: Yes.

Counselor: So back to the idea of doing a volunteers job. I know this was a goal of yours from the start.

Client: Yes it was. I don't feel too far off. It doesn't feel like it's too far away, me being able to do an odd hour here and there if they'll let me. They might want me to come in at a set time so I will need to speak to the different places to find one where I can just pop in now and again to begin with.

Counselor: Good idea. I know you said that once you were able to go in to town for an hour or so, you would probably be ready to start volunteering.

Client: Yes.

Counselor: Is there anything else that could help you feel ready to volunteer? What would make volunteering easier for you?

(I have in the back of my mind that the client said that once she was ready to start working, even if was volunteering, she would be ready to finish the sessions. I am beginning to wonder if this will be our last session.)

Client: I'm not sure.

Counselor: Okay, how would you get to the volunteer job?

Client: Well I would chose somewhere local and I just thought I'd walk. I'd be able to walk there.

Counselor: Okay.

Client: Oh, maybe I could drive?

Counselor: Let's compare the two. Let's imagine that you are going to walk to the volunteer job and volunteer for one hour. How ready do you feel to do that? 0 being not ready at all and 10 being ready.

Client: A 4.

Counselor: Now let's consider you drive to the volunteer's job and you volunteer for one hour. How ready do you feel to do that? 0 being not ready at all and 10 being ready?

Client: Probably a 7 or even an 8. It's no different to me driving to my Mum's house and staying there for an hour.

Counselor: Is a 7 or an 8 high enough for you try volunteering now?

Client: Yes it is. I'm ready to try it now if I drive! I can't believe I'm saying that but if it's only for an hour and I can drive, I think it's within my capabilities now. I could do it.

Counselor: So what do you need to do to make that happen?

(I want the client to develop a concrete plan. If she has it planned out in her mind, it might be easier for her to take action on it.)

Client: I could make a list of the places I would like to volunteer and give them a ring. I'd ask to speak to the manager to discuss my anxiety, my situation. I could start with the place I would like to volunteer at the most and then work down the list. I would mention that initially I would work sporadically and then hopefully I could start planning hours when I felt a little more comfortable. That could work couldn't it?

Counselor: Yes, I think so.

Client: I think that's what I need to do. I need to try and find ways of doing things that are comfortable for me. Think of the different options. It's like having Mum on stand-by when I walked to the shop. It just made it easier. It gave me more confidence. With this situation it's taking the car rather than walking.

Counselor: I think it's really impressive the way that you are recognizing that you can sometimes make situations easier for yourself. If it feels too difficult, you can look at some ways to make it easier and therefore make you feel more confident. You went from not feeling confident volunteering at the start of this session to realizing that you could actually volunteer if you only did the odd hour here and there and drove.

Client: That's right. I think I am getting some really good strategies together now.

Counselor: We spoke in the first session about how we will know that our time together has finished. You mentioned that you felt the sessions could end once you felt ready to work, even if it was a volunteer role.

Client: I did, didn't I? Do you think that I am ready to stop the sessions? I've only had 5 I think.

Counselor: The average number of sessions is 4 or 5. Some people have longer than this maybe 12 sessions and others will only have one session. It really depends on the person.

Client: So I don't need to keep seeing you until I actually get rid of all of my anxiety?

Counselor: No, not unless you feel it would help you. As long as you feel that you have everything you need to achieve your goal and feel happy to finish the sessions. I don't need to be there at the end to see you achieve your goal.

Client: I do kind of feel that way. I feel like I know what I am doing. I think I know how to think about things so even if I do have a setback, I know how to deal with it. I think I also know how to come up with my own strategies. Analyze the situation. Look at what worked.

Counselor: That's right. So would you like another session or do you wish to stop the sessions? You can of course call me up at any point in the future to have another session if you feel you need it.

Client: I think I'm happy to stop the sessions today. I can see how I get on and if I reach a point where I can't get any further I can give you a call?

Counselor: Yes of course. What might make you reach a point where you can't get any further?

Client: I don't know. I worry that I can only get so far.

Counselor: What makes you think that?

Client: Well, I can't imagine being able to go to London for example.

Counselor: Is there anything that you used to think that way about that you can now do?

Client: Well yes! I suppose there is! I can drive to my friends' houses and my Mums house now. I've been in a shop in the city. They are all things I couldn't imagine myself doing a few months back.

Counselor: So what does that tell you?

Client: That I can probably do it!

Counselor: Great. Is there anything you would like to discuss in the remainder of this session? Anything that you think we should talk about? Anything that we have not covered?

Client: No, not that I can think of. We have pretty much covered everything.

Counselor: Great. If it's okay I would like to just talk briefly about maintaining your good work?

Client: Yes, okay that's fine.

Counselor: So everything is going great for you at the moment. You have your strategies in place that work for you. You are taking small steps and progressing nicely towards your goals.

Client: Yes.

Counselor: How will you remember what to do when you feel discouraged?

(I want the client to be as fully prepared as possible. I want her to think through the times when things might not go so well. I want her to able to recognize these moments quickly and implement a plan straight away.)

Client: I think I know that I have come quite far recently. I would just remind myself of that. I think that I would also continue to note everything down in my notebook. I will carry on noting down stuff each time I go out, what I was thinking and feeling and so on. That way if I do experience a setback and start to feel discouraged I can look at what I was thinking or feeling and see where I was going wrong. It might be that I have started to focus on myself failing again rather than succeeding. Like I did last month, until I noticed.

Counselor: That's a good plan. So you will continue to use your notes to monitor what is helping and not helping?

Client: Yes.

Counselor: What would be the first signs to you that were starting to feel discouraged?

Client: I would feel tearful and probably annoyed at myself. I'd start feeling like I had let myself down.

Counselor: And what would you do at that point?

Client: I'd probably just take a few hours to relax and then I'd look through my notes. Remind myself how well I'm doing.

Counselor: Great. How do you think other people will respond as you continue to make these changes and progress towards your goals?

(I want the client to be feeling motivated at the end of our session so want her to think through how other people will react.)

Client: I think they'll be happy. Pleased for me. Rob seemed a little bit off with me when I mentioned that maybe I could start volunteering soon. I don't know why but a small part of me wondered if he was anxious about me getting out and about and meeting people again. He always was the jealous type.

Counselor: How will you manage that?

Client: I don't think there is a lot I can do about it really. I will just try to reassure him and make him feel secure.

Counselor: How will you ensure that you carry on towards your goals if Rob appears to be displaying signs of jealously?

Client: Oh, I won't let it stop me. I'm not giving up my health for that! No way! I will just carry on. He'll get used to it. I used to work and he dealt with it then so he can deal with it again. It shouldn't be a problem really. I hope that he supports me as I continue to get better. He always said he wanted me to get better.

Counselor: So if you notice that Rob is starting to feel jealous, you will try to reassure him and make him feel secure. You will carry on working towards your goals.

Client: Yes definitely. I'm sure he'll be fine.

(My attempt at motivating the client actually resulted in the revelation of a potential obstacle. I am hoping to ask another motivating question before we finish the session if it feels appropriate.)

Counselor: Right, is there anything you would like to discuss or shall we draw this session to a close?

Client: No, I can't think of anything. Like I said before I think it's all about the doing for me now.

Counselor: Good.

Client: I was just thinking once I start to volunteer, I must make sure that I continue to try and progress my goals. Like once I start volunteering for an odd hour here or there, I need to work towards increasing my hours, then maybe getting a paid part-time job, then moving to a full-time job. I must remember to keep pushing myself. Not get lazy. Not get comfortable and think I've done enough now.

Counselor: How will you do that?

Client: I don't know. I don't think that I would let myself get lazy. But what if I do?

Counselor: What would the benefits be to you if you keep on striving for the next goal?

Client: I'm not sure.

Counselor: Okay, let me put it another way. You mentioned that one of the goals further down the road is for you to have a full time job. What would the benefits be to you if you had a full time job?

Client: Oh wow, it would be so much better. I'd be able to buy new clothes when I wanted, maybe buy a new car, I wouldn't have to worry about money anymore. I'd be able to pay my way with the bills rather than relying on Rob. I could even go on holiday.

Counselor: What difference would that make to you?

Client: Such a difference! I would feel like I was a normal person again. That I'd made it to the finish line. That I'd had anxiety and I had recovered from it totally. I'd be completely me again.

Counselor: Will there be a benefit to anyone else?

Client: Yes, to everyone I know. I'd be able to go to all of their birthday do's and weddings. Me and Rob would be able to go on holiday like a normal couple. We could go on days out to the beach and stuff like that that. I could take mum and dad out for day trips. I think everyone would benefit. It would be great.

Counselor: So if you were to continue working on your goals, progressing through them, you would benefit and your family and friends would benefit.

Client: Yes, I think there would be massive benefits for everyone. That makes me feel even more motivated, even more like I want this!

Counselor: Great. Anything else you would like to talk about?

Client: Nope.

Counselor: Okay, well as before I will just have a look through my notes and I'll feedback to you on what we have covered this session.

Client: Okay.

Counselor looks through notes.

Counselor: Firstly, I would like to say how impressed I am at how much you have achieved in this last month. Even though you have had the occasional set back you were able to overcome this quickly by reminding yourself how far you'd come. You also looked at your notes to consider how you were thinking and feeling and were able to spot what was helping and what was not helping. I think is really resourceful of you.

There have been times when you have been out and feeling anxious and you have managed to remain in the situation. Even though you were feeling anxious you remembered your strategy of reminding yourself that even if you did have a panic attack, the first one would be the worst and the rest would be less intense.

We spoke about the possibility of you volunteering and you felt able to consider doing it if you were able to volunteer for an hour here or there and drove to the volunteer job. You said you could phone around the different places you wanted to volunteer at and discuss your situation with them. It helped to think of different ways of approaching the volunteering goal to make the goal feel easier and more comfortable for you.

We also spoke about starting to plan your activities. You mentioned that you wanted to plan to walk 10 steps from your drive tomorrow morning.

Client: Yes.

Counselor: You had the idea of building up the planned activities much like you did with the spontaneous activities by using small steps that you felt capable of doing. We spoke about the possibility of having a full-time job in the future and how that would benefit you and your life, and the lives of your family and friends.

Client: Yes, that would make a massive difference to everyone.

Counselor: We have agreed that this is your last session today as you feel that you have all the strategies you need and it is about action now.

Client: That's right.

Counselor: How does that all feel to you?

Client: Yea good. Oh I forgot to tell you that I made a note of all the strategies I have been using. To be honest I don't look at it much as I know what they are now. I've practiced them so much. And reading through my notes looking for what helps and what doesn't, keeps reinforcing the strategies.

Counselor: That's fine. It's good that you are able to recognize what you can stop doing and what you want to keep doing. You are able to work out what works for you.

Client: Yes.

(Even though we have not had a full length session there is no point in dragging the session out for the sake of it. I would rather the client left when they were feeling motivated and ready to carry on working towards their goals.)

Counselor: So, that's the end of the session. I wish you all the best in the future. I am sure that you will be fine but if you would like a follow up session at any point, please just call.

Client: Thank you. You've really helped.

(I really need the client to appreciate that it was them that had all the solutions not me.)

Counselor: It was you that did all the hard work. It was you that came up with all the solutions that work for you.

Client: Yea, I guess I did!

Counselor: I'll walk you out.

Counseling session ends.

More books by this author

The Counseling Sessions: Overcoming Low Mood and Depression

The Counseling Sessions: Overcoming Feelings of Irritability and Anger in Relationships

How to Manage Stress in the Workplace: The No Waffle Guide for Managers (EBook Only)

How to Manage Teams: The No Waffle Guide to Managing Your Team Effectively

Presentation Skills: Portraying Confidence, Answering Tricky Questions and Structuring Content

Change Management for Managers: The No Waffle Guide to Managing Change in the Workplace

How to Manage People: The No Waffle Guide to Managing Performance, Change and Stress in the Workplace

Manager's Guide to Providing Feedback: The No Waffle Guide to Providing Feedback and Rewards (EBook Only)

Coaching Skills for Managers: The No Waffle Guide to Getting the Best from Your Team (EBook Only)

What Other Marketing Books Won't Tell You: A Brutally Honest Account of Marketing a Small Business

CPSIA information can be obtained
at www.ICGtesting.com
Printed in the USA
LVHW111505281020
670060LV00023B/340

9 781074 951122